GOSCINNY AND UDERZO

PRESENT

AN ASTERIX ADVENTURE

University of the
West of England

BRISTOL

**EDUCATION
RESOURCES
CENTRE**

This book should be returned by the last date
stamped below.

UWE, BRISTOL   B1084.03.01
Printing & Stationery Services

a division of Hodder Headline plc

Asterix and the Black Gold

Original edition © Les editions Albert René, Goscinny-Uderzo, 1981
English translation: © Les Editions Albert René, Goscinny-Uderzo, 1982
Exclusive licensee: Hodder and Stoughton Ltd
Translators: Anthea Bell and Derek Hockridge

First published in Great Britain 1982 (cased)

This impression: 1995 1996 1997 1998

ISBN 0 340 38841 2

1859984088

Published by Hodder Children's Books,
a division of Hodder Headline plc
338 Euston Road, London NW1 3BH

Printed in Belgium by Proost International Book Production

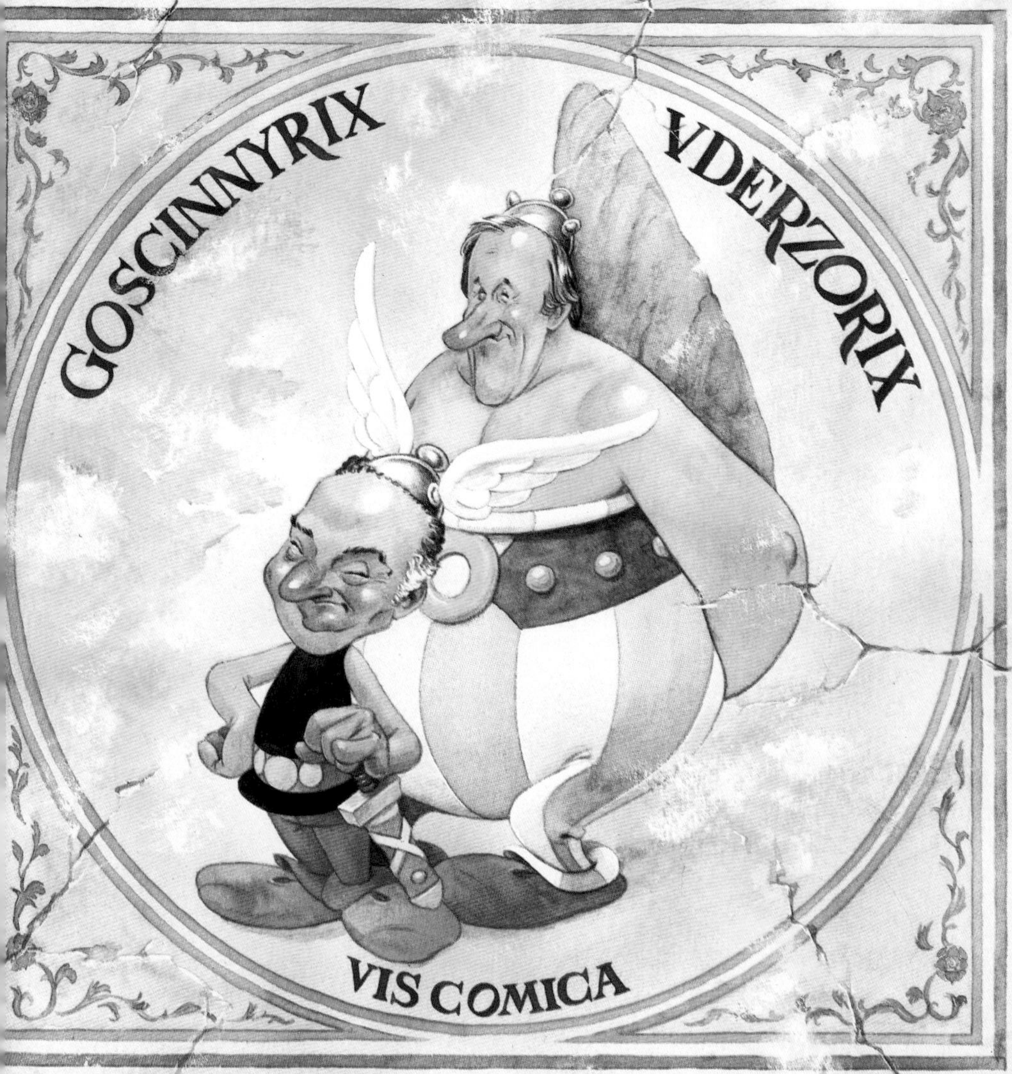
GOSCINNYRIX
VDERZORIX
VIS COMICA

he power to make people laugh: from an epigram by Caesar on Terence, the Latin poet.

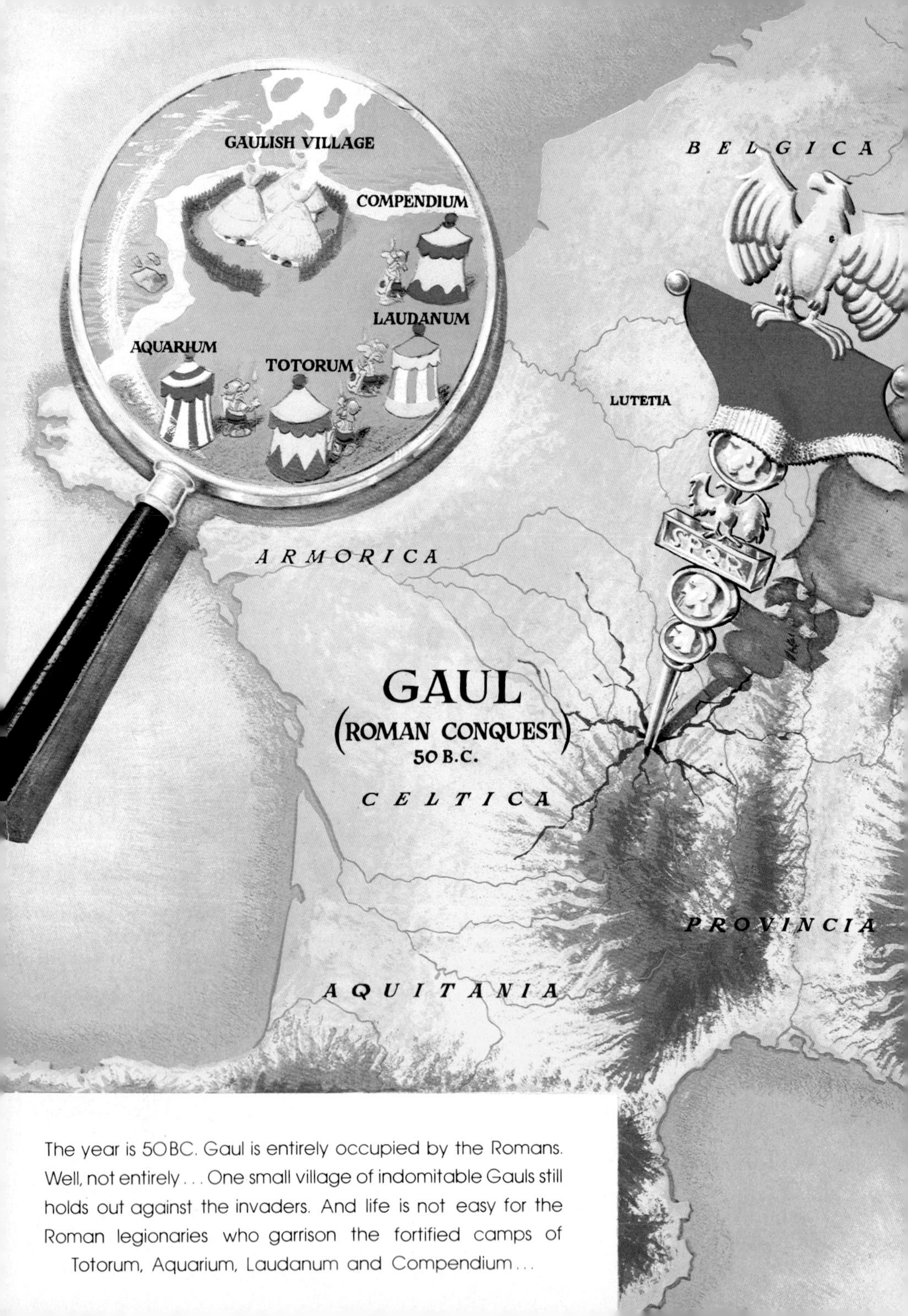
GAULISH VILLAGE
COMPENDIUM
LAUDANUM
AQUARIUM
TOTORUM
BELGICA
LUTETIA
SPQR
ARMORICA
GAUL
(ROMAN CONQUEST)
50 B.C.
CELTICA
PROVINCIA
AQUITANIA

The year is 50BC. Gaul is entirely occupied by the Romans. Well, not entirely . . . One small village of indomitable Gauls still holds out against the invaders. And life is not easy for the Roman legionaries who garrison the fortified camps of Totorum, Aquarium, Laudanum and Compendium . . .

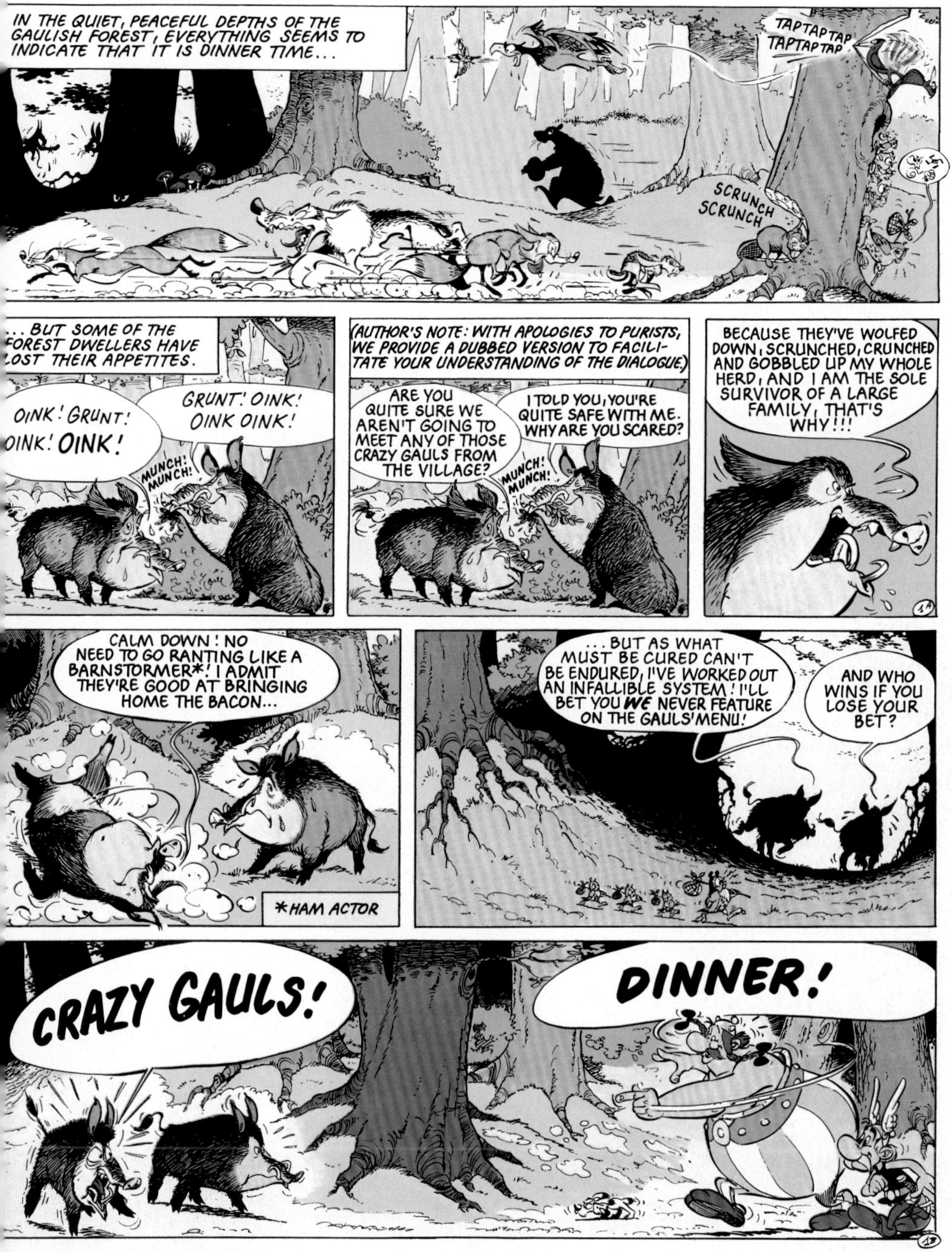

IN THE QUIET, PEACEFUL DEPTHS OF THE GAULISH FOREST, EVERYTHING SEEMS TO INDICATE THAT IT IS DINNER TIME...
TAPTAPTAP TAPTAPTAP
SCRUNCH SCRUNCH
... BUT SOME OF THE FOREST DWELLERS HAVE LOST THEIR APPETITES.
OINK! GRUNT! OINK! OINK!
GRUNT! OINK! OINK OINK!
MUNCH! MUNCH!
(AUTHOR'S NOTE: WITH APOLOGIES TO PURISTS, WE PROVIDE A DUBBED VERSION TO FACILITATE YOUR UNDERSTANDING OF THE DIALOGUE)
ARE YOU QUITE SURE WE AREN'T GOING TO MEET ANY OF THOSE CRAZY GAULS FROM THE VILLAGE?
I TOLD YOU, YOU'RE QUITE SAFE WITH ME. WHY ARE YOU SCARED?
MUNCH! MUNCH!
BECAUSE THEY'VE WOLFED DOWN, SCRUNCHED, CRUNCHED AND GOBBLED UP MY WHOLE HERD, AND I AM THE SOLE SURVIVOR OF A LARGE FAMILY, THAT'S WHY!!!
CALM DOWN! NO NEED TO GO RANTING LIKE A BARNSTORMER*! I ADMIT THEY'RE GOOD AT BRINGING HOME THE BACON...
*HAM ACTOR
... BUT AS WHAT MUST BE CURED CAN'T BE ENDURED, I'VE WORKED OUT AN INFALLIBLE SYSTEM! I'LL BET YOU WE NEVER FEATURE ON THE GAULS' MENU!
AND WHO WINS IF YOU LOSE YOUR BET?
CRAZY GAULS!
DINNER!

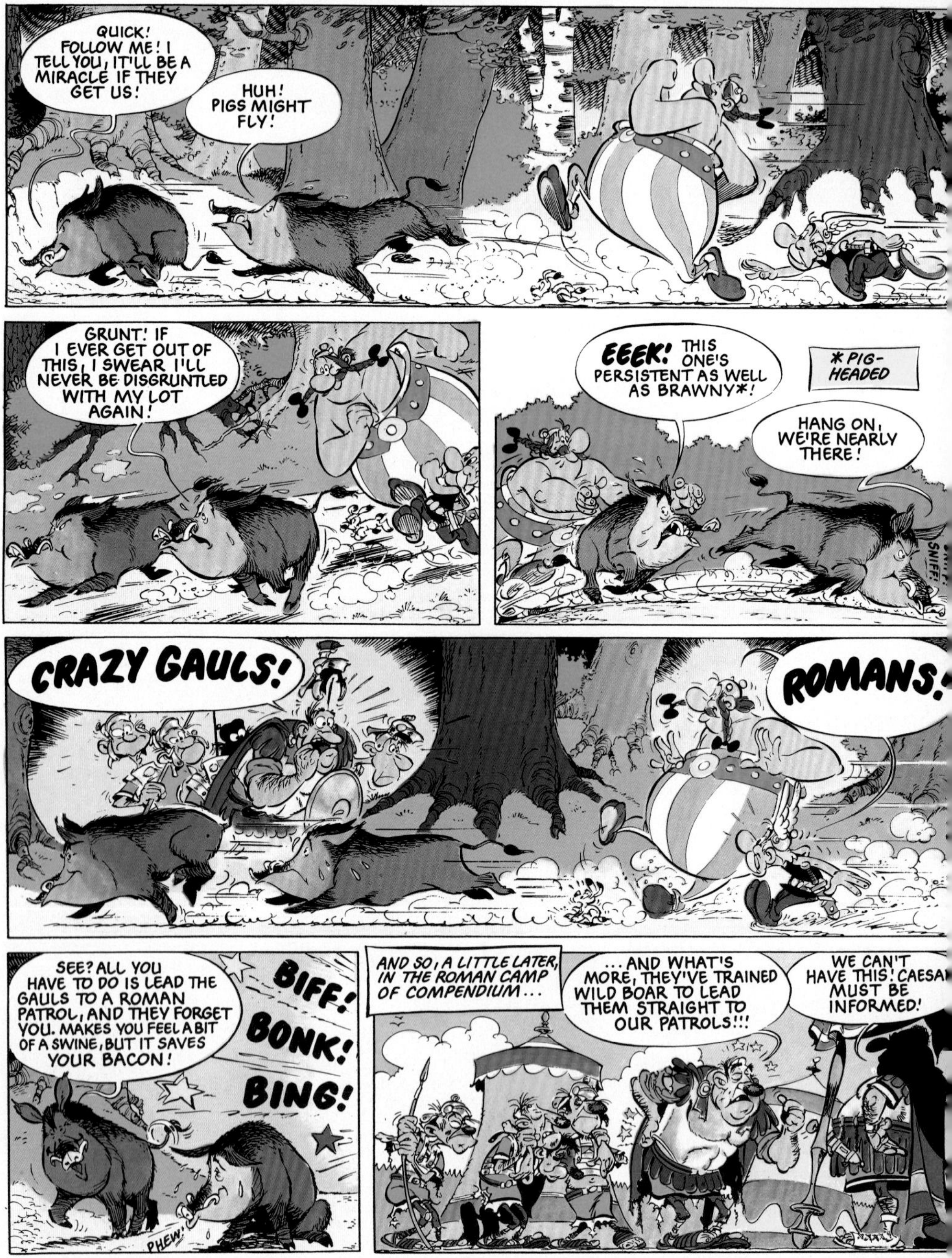
QUICK! FOLLOW ME! I TELL YOU, IT'LL BE A MIRACLE IF THEY GET US!
HUH! PIGS MIGHT FLY!
GRUNT! IF I EVER GET OUT OF THIS, I SWEAR I'LL NEVER BE DISGRUNTLED WITH MY LOT AGAIN!
EEEK! THIS ONE'S PERSISTENT AS WELL AS BRAWNY*!
* PIG-HEADED
HANG ON, WE'RE NEARLY THERE!
SNIFF!
CRAZY GAULS!
ROMANS!
SEE? ALL YOU HAVE TO DO IS LEAD THE GAULS TO A ROMAN PATROL, AND THEY FORGET YOU. MAKES YOU FEEL A BIT OF A SWINE, BUT IT SAVES YOUR BACON!
BIFF!
BONK!
BING!
PHEW!
AND SO, A LITTLE LATER, IN THE ROMAN CAMP OF COMPENDIUM...
...AND WHAT'S MORE, THEY'VE TRAINED WILD BOAR TO LEAD THEM STRAIGHT TO OUR PATROLS!!!
WE CAN'T HAVE THIS! CAESA[R] MUST BE INFORMED!

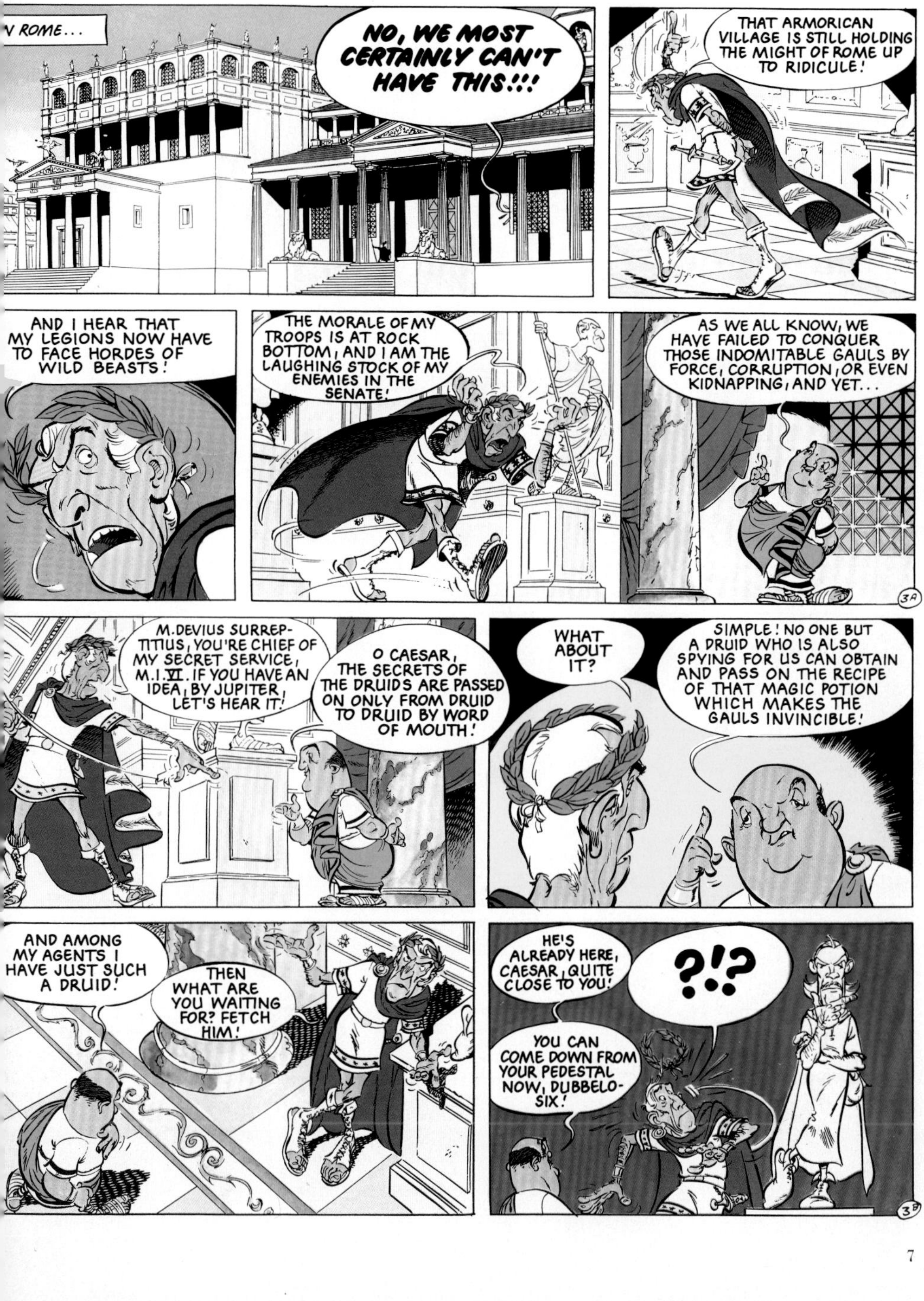
N ROME...
NO, WE MOST CERTAINLY CAN'T HAVE THIS!!!
THAT ARMORICAN VILLAGE IS STILL HOLDING THE MIGHT OF ROME UP TO RIDICULE!
AND I HEAR THAT MY LEGIONS NOW HAVE TO FACE HORDES OF WILD BEASTS!
THE MORALE OF MY TROOPS IS AT ROCK BOTTOM, AND I AM THE LAUGHING STOCK OF MY ENEMIES IN THE SENATE!
AS WE ALL KNOW, WE HAVE FAILED TO CONQUER THOSE INDOMITABLE GAULS BY FORCE, CORRUPTION, OR EVEN KIDNAPPING, AND YET...
3A
M. DEVIUS SURREPTITIUS, YOU'RE CHIEF OF MY SECRET SERVICE, M.I.VI. IF YOU HAVE AN IDEA, BY JUPITER, LET'S HEAR IT!
O CAESAR, THE SECRETS OF THE DRUIDS ARE PASSED ON ONLY FROM DRUID TO DRUID BY WORD OF MOUTH!
WHAT ABOUT IT?
SIMPLE! NO ONE BUT A DRUID WHO IS ALSO SPYING FOR US CAN OBTAIN AND PASS ON THE RECIPE OF THAT MAGIC POTION WHICH MAKES THE GAULS INVINCIBLE!
AND AMONG MY AGENTS I HAVE JUST SUCH A DRUID!
THEN WHAT ARE YOU WAITING FOR? FETCH HIM!
HE'S ALREADY HERE, CAESAR, QUITE CLOSE TO YOU!
?!?
YOU CAN COME DOWN FROM YOUR PEDESTAL NOW, DUBBELOSIX!
3B

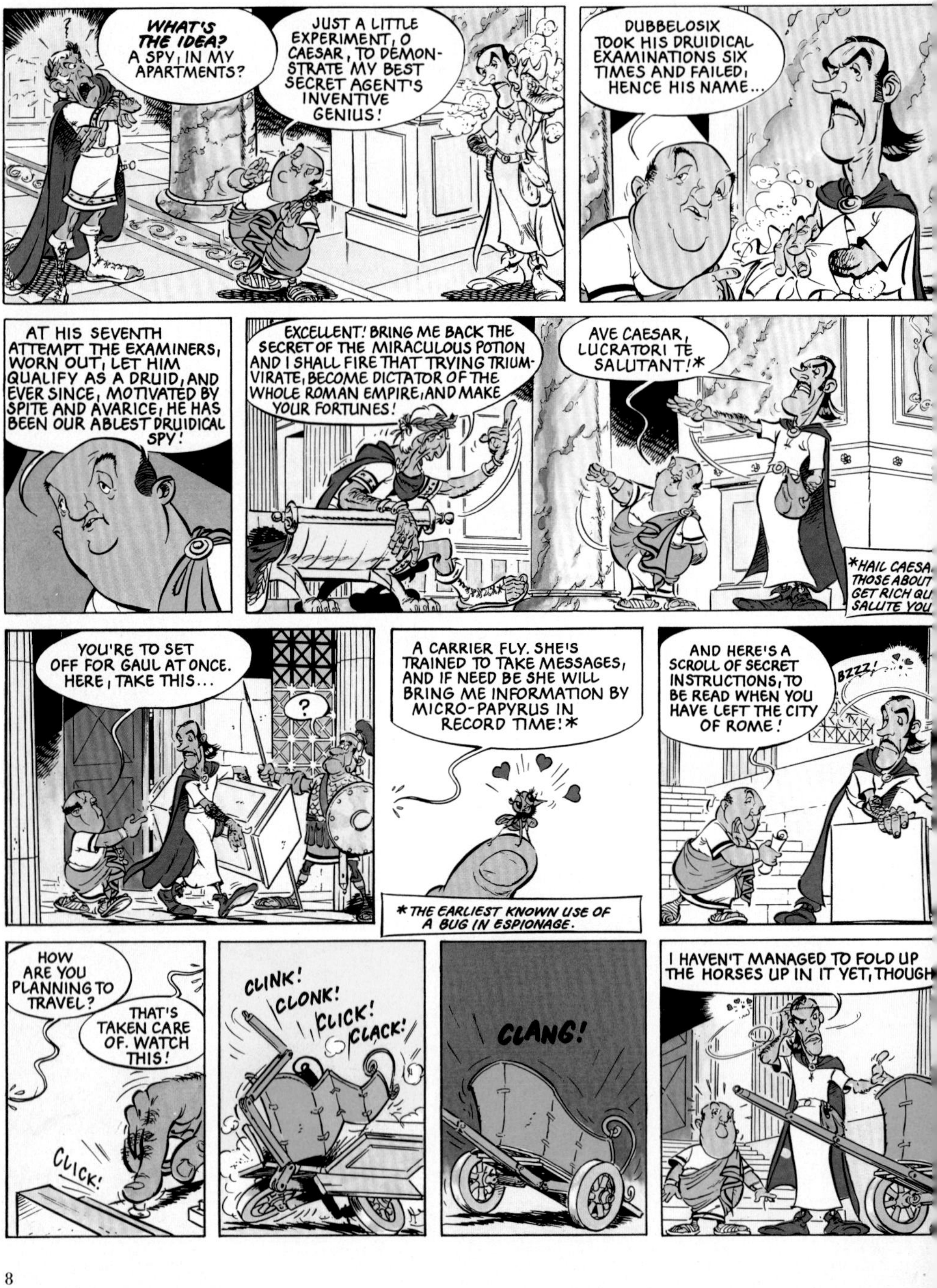
WHAT'S THE IDEA? A SPY, IN MY APARTMENTS?
JUST A LITTLE EXPERIMENT, O CAESAR, TO DEMONSTRATE MY BEST SECRET AGENT'S INVENTIVE GENIUS!
DUBBELOSIX TOOK HIS DRUIDICAL EXAMINATIONS SIX TIMES AND FAILED, HENCE HIS NAME...
AT HIS SEVENTH ATTEMPT THE EXAMINERS, WORN OUT, LET HIM QUALIFY AS A DRUID, AND EVER SINCE, MOTIVATED BY SPITE AND AVARICE, HE HAS BEEN OUR ABLEST DRUIDICAL SPY!
EXCELLENT! BRING ME BACK THE SECRET OF THE MIRACULOUS POTION AND I SHALL FIRE THAT TRYING TRIUMVIRATE, BECOME DICTATOR OF THE WHOLE ROMAN EMPIRE, AND MAKE YOUR FORTUNES!
AVE CAESAR, LUCRATORI TE SALUTANT!*
*HAIL CAESA
THOSE ABOUT
GET RICH QU
SALUTE YOU
YOU'RE TO SET OFF FOR GAUL AT ONCE. HERE, TAKE THIS...
?
A CARRIER FLY. SHE'S TRAINED TO TAKE MESSAGES, AND IF NEED BE SHE WILL BRING ME INFORMATION BY MICRO-PAPYRUS IN RECORD TIME!*
*THE EARLIEST KNOWN USE OF A BUG IN ESPIONAGE.
AND HERE'S A SCROLL OF SECRET INSTRUCTIONS, TO BE READ WHEN YOU HAVE LEFT THE CITY OF ROME!
BZZZ!
HOW ARE YOU PLANNING TO TRAVEL?
THAT'S TAKEN CARE OF. WATCH THIS!
CLICK!
CLINK!
CLONK!
CLICK!
CLACK!
CLANG!
I HAVEN'T MANAGED TO FOLD UP THE HORSES UP IN IT YET, THOUGH

LATER...

WHOA!

TIME TO READ SURREPTITIUS'S SECRET INSTRUCTIONS!

BZZZZ!

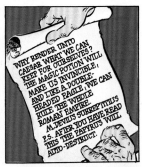

WHY RENDER UNTO CAESAR WHAT WE CAN KEEP FOR OURSELVES? THE MAGIC POTION WILL MAKE US INVINCIBLE, AND LIKE A DOUBLE-HEADED EAGLE, WE CAN RULE THE WHOLE ROMAN EMPIRE.
M. DEVIUS SURREPTITIUS

P.S. AFTER YOU HAVE READ THIS, THE PAPYRUS WILL AUTO-DESTRUCT.

?!

PSSCHCH CH...

HO, HO! CAESAR AND SURREPTITIUS ARE A COUPLE OF FOOLS! I PLAN TO BE A VULTURE RULING THE GALLO-ROMAN EMPIRE ALONE!

BZZZZ

KISS!

OH LEAVE ME ALONE, YOU WRETCHED CREATURE!

BZZZZ Z Z

5A

MEANWHILE, ON THE ARMORICAN COAST, ALL IS PEACEFUL IN THE LITTLE GAULISH VILLAGE WHERE ASTERIX AND HIS FRIENDS LIVE.

IT'S A FUNNY THING, BUT WHEN WE GO WILD BOAR-HUNTING THESE DAYS WE KEEP FINDING ROMAN PATROLS!

YES, YOU'D THINK THEY'D KNOW BY NOW BOAR IS ONE OF OUR SACRED COWS!
SCRUNCH!

AND YOU CERTAINLY GO THE WHOLE HOG EATING IT!

SCRUNCH! MUNCH! SCRUNCH!

5B

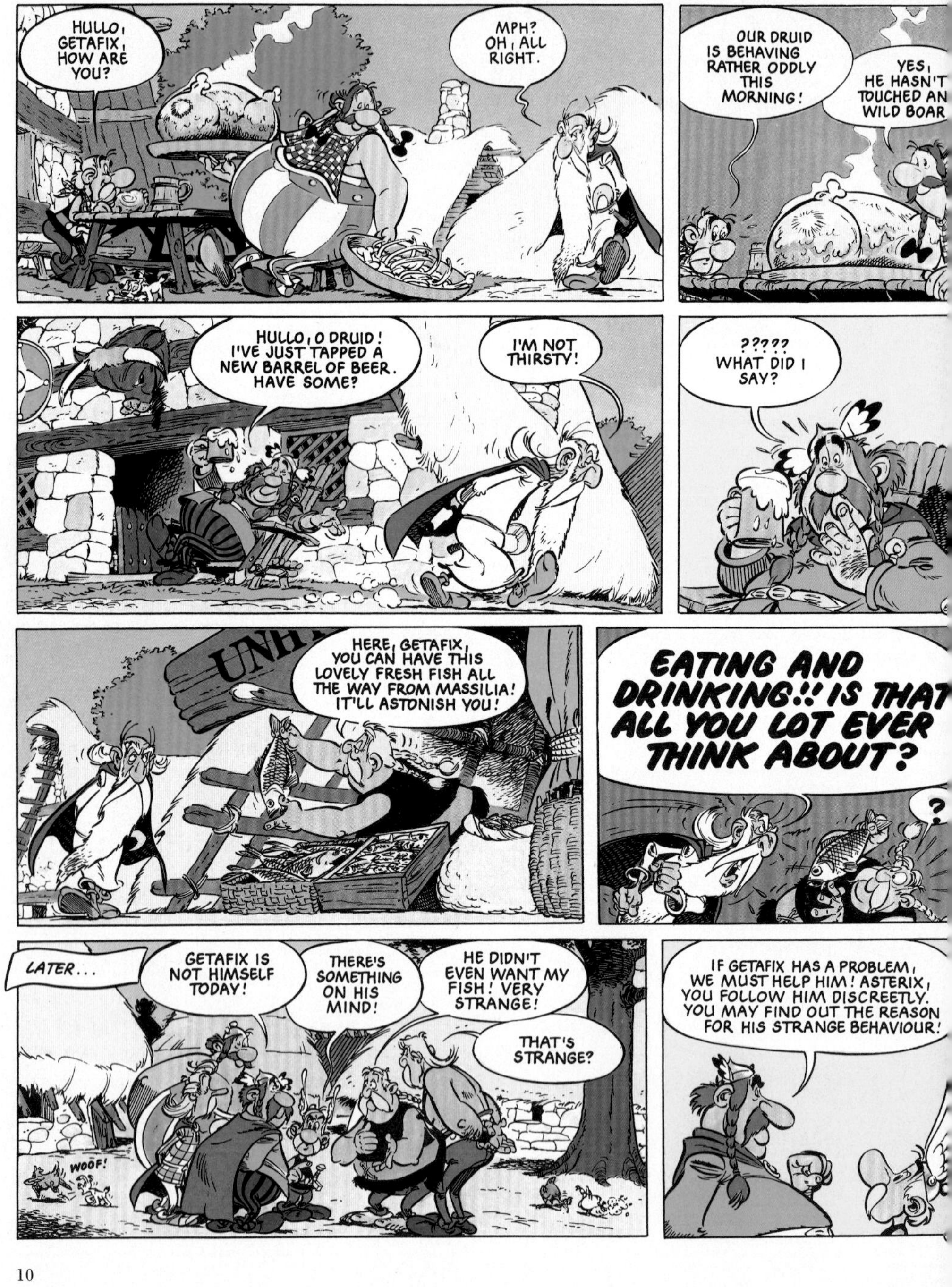
HULLO, GETAFIX, HOW ARE YOU?
MPH? OH, ALL RIGHT.
OUR DRUID IS BEHAVING RATHER ODDLY THIS MORNING!
YES, HE HASN'T TOUCHED AN WILD BOAR
HULLO, O DRUID! I'VE JUST TAPPED A NEW BARREL OF BEER. HAVE SOME?
I'M NOT THIRSTY!
????? WHAT DID I SAY?
HERE, GETAFIX, YOU CAN HAVE THIS LOVELY FRESH FISH ALL THE WAY FROM MASSILIA! IT'LL ASTONISH YOU!
EATING AND DRINKING!! IS THAT ALL YOU LOT EVER THINK ABOUT?
?
LATER...
GETAFIX IS NOT HIMSELF TODAY!
THERE'S SOMETHING ON HIS MIND!
HE DIDN'T EVEN WANT MY FISH! VERY STRANGE!
THAT'S STRANGE?
WOOF!
IF GETAFIX HAS A PROBLEM, WE MUST HELP HIM! ASTERIX, YOU FOLLOW HIM DISCREETLY. YOU MAY FIND OUT THE REASON FOR HIS STRANGE BEHAVIOUR!

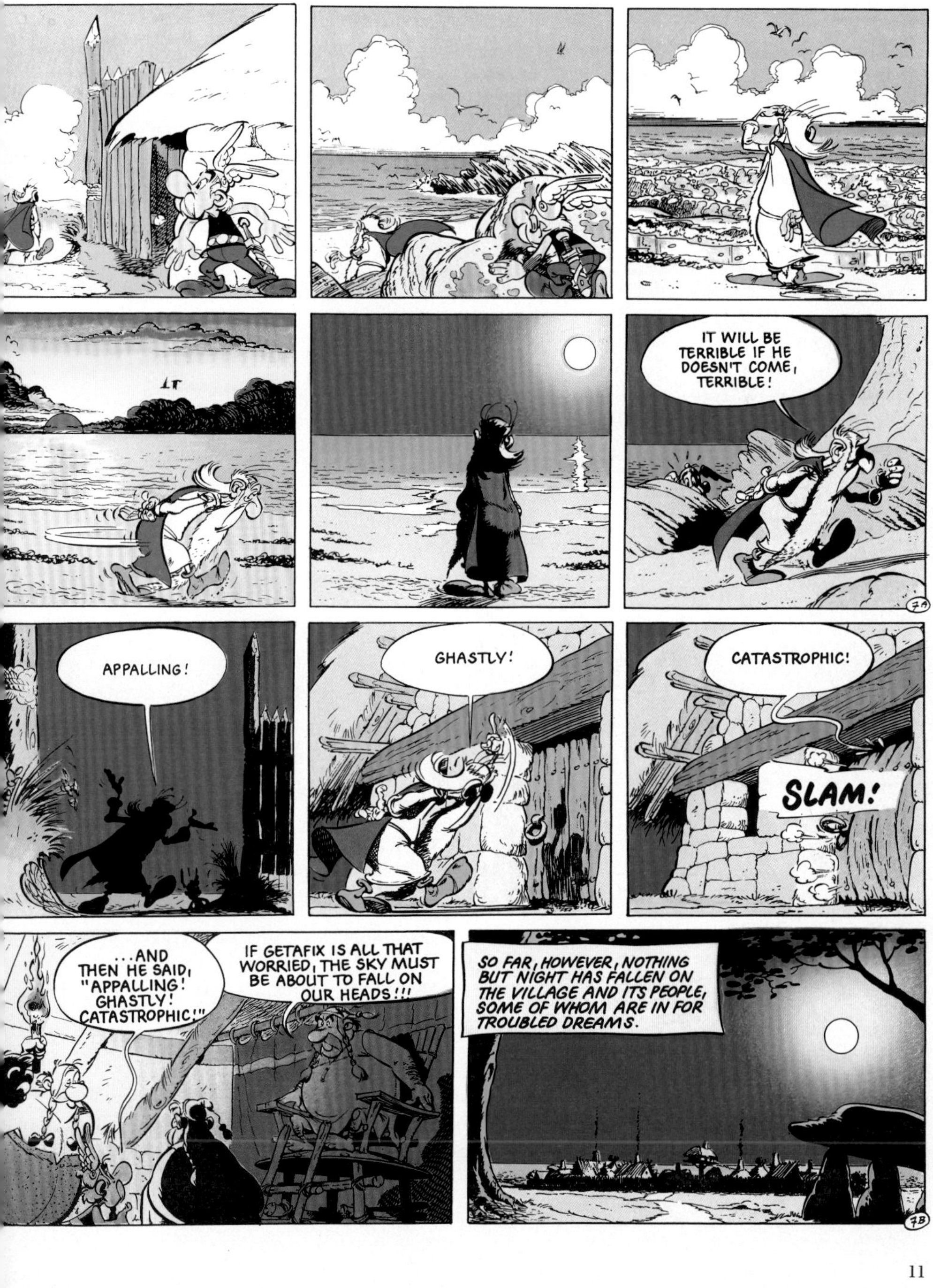
IT WILL BE TERRIBLE IF HE DOESN'T COME, TERRIBLE!
7A
APPALLING!
GHASTLY!
CATASTROPHIC!
SLAM!
...AND THEN HE SAID, "APPALLING! GHASTLY! CATASTROPHIC!"
IF GETAFIX IS ALL THAT WORRIED, THE SKY MUST BE ABOUT TO FALL ON OUR HEADS!!!
SO FAR, HOWEVER, NOTHING BUT NIGHT HAS FALLEN ON THE VILLAGE AND ITS PEOPLE, SOME OF WHOM ARE IN FOR TROUBLED DREAMS.
7B

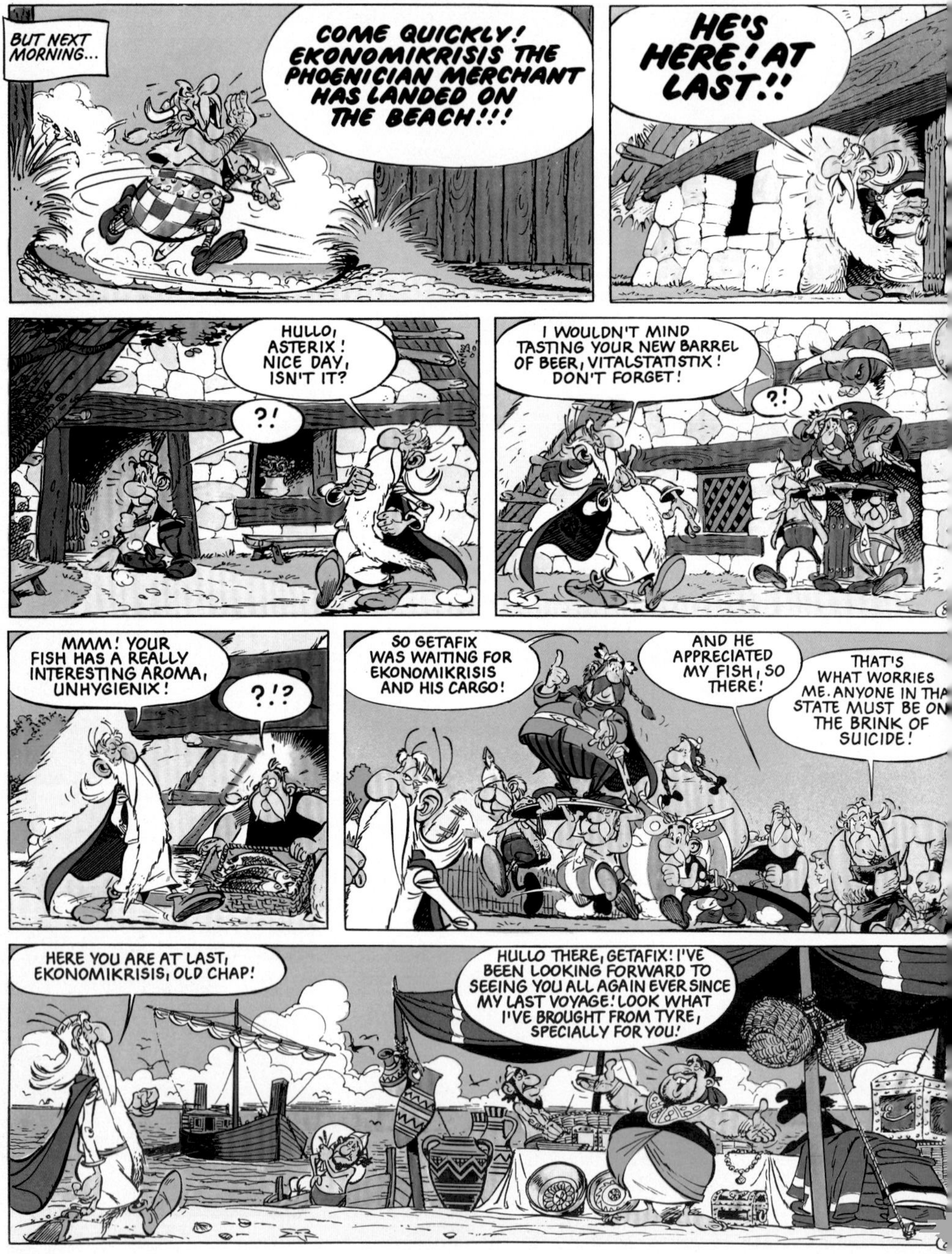
BUT NEXT MORNING...
COME QUICKLY! EKONOMIKRISIS THE PHOENICIAN MERCHANT HAS LANDED ON THE BEACH!!!
HE'S HERE! AT LAST!!
HULLO, ASTERIX! NICE DAY, ISN'T IT?
?!
I WOULDN'T MIND TASTING YOUR NEW BARREL OF BEER, VITALSTATISTIX! DON'T FORGET!
?!
MMM! YOUR FISH HAS A REALLY INTERESTING AROMA, UNHYGIENIX!
?!?
SO GETAFIX WAS WAITING FOR EKONOMIKRISIS AND HIS CARGO!
AND HE APPRECIATED MY FISH, SO THERE!
THAT'S WHAT WORRIES ME. ANYONE IN THA STATE MUST BE ON THE BRINK OF SUICIDE!
HERE YOU ARE AT LAST, EKONOMIKRISIS, OLD CHAP!
HULLO THERE, GETAFIX! I'VE BEEN LOOKING FORWARD TO SEEING YOU ALL AGAIN EVER SINCE MY LAST VOYAGE! LOOK WHAT I'VE BROUGHT FROM TYRE, SPECIALLY FOR YOU!

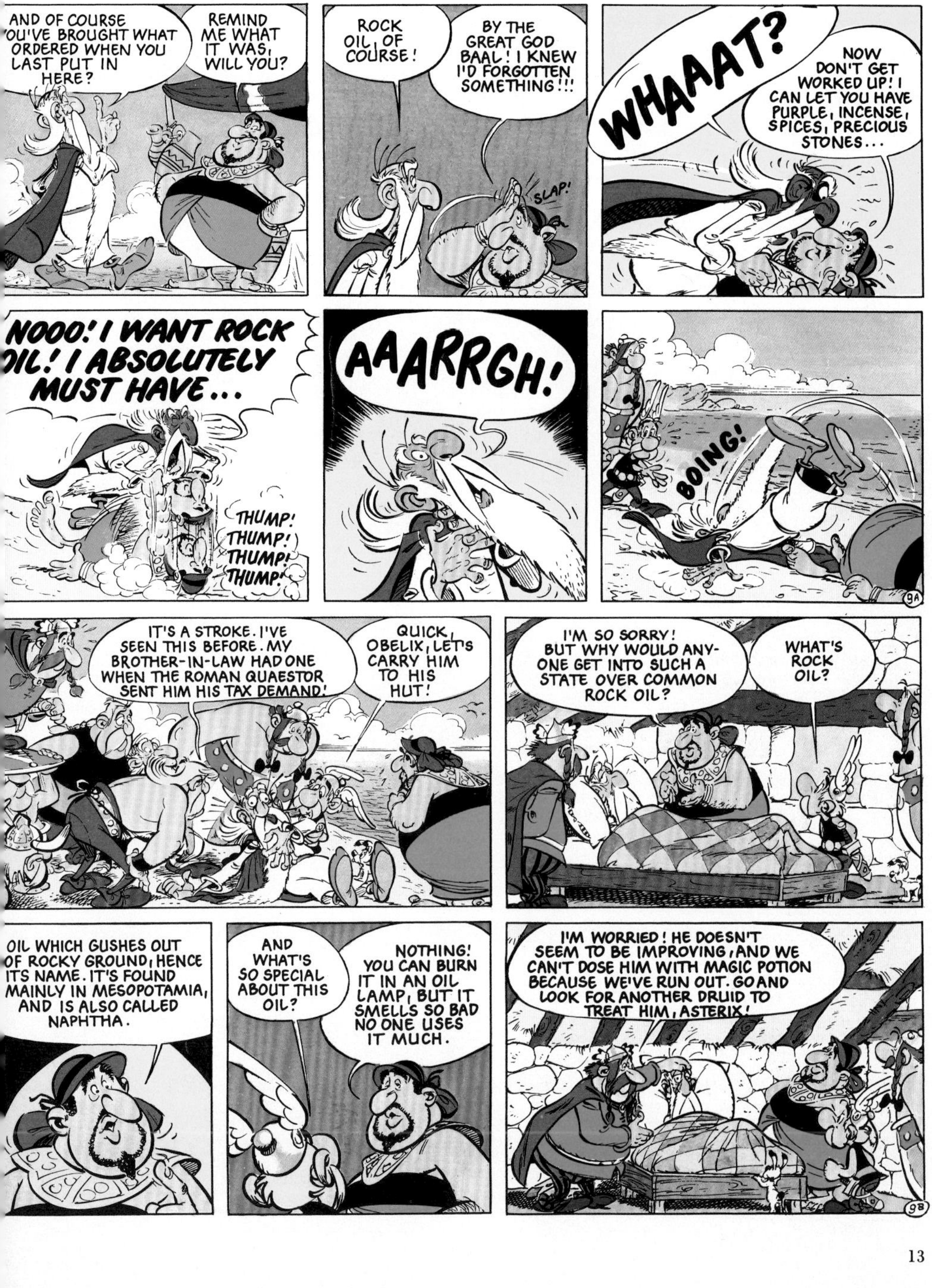

AND OF COURSE YOU'VE BROUGHT WHAT I ORDERED WHEN YOU LAST PUT IN HERE?
REMIND ME WHAT IT WAS, WILL YOU?
ROCK OIL, OF COURSE!
BY THE GREAT GOD BAAL! I KNEW I'D FORGOTTEN SOMETHING!!!
SLAP!
WHAAAT?
NOW DON'T GET WORKED UP! I CAN LET YOU HAVE PURPLE, INCENSE, SPICES, PRECIOUS STONES...
NOOO! I WANT ROCK OIL! I ABSOLUTELY MUST HAVE...
THUMP! THUMP! THUMP! THUMP!
AAARRGH!
BOING!
IT'S A STROKE. I'VE SEEN THIS BEFORE. MY BROTHER-IN-LAW HAD ONE WHEN THE ROMAN QUAESTOR SENT HIM HIS TAX DEMAND!
QUICK, OBELIX, LET'S CARRY HIM TO HIS HUT!
I'M SO SORRY! BUT WHY WOULD ANYONE GET INTO SUCH A STATE OVER COMMON ROCK OIL?
WHAT'S ROCK OIL?
OIL WHICH GUSHES OUT OF ROCKY GROUND, HENCE ITS NAME. IT'S FOUND MAINLY IN MESOPOTAMIA, AND IS ALSO CALLED NAPHTHA.
AND WHAT'S SO SPECIAL ABOUT THIS OIL?
NOTHING! YOU CAN BURN IT IN AN OIL LAMP, BUT IT SMELLS SO BAD NO ONE USES IT MUCH.
I'M WORRIED! HE DOESN'T SEEM TO BE IMPROVING, AND WE CAN'T DOSE HIM WITH MAGIC POTION BECAUSE WE'VE RUN OUT. GO AND LOOK FOR ANOTHER DRUID TO TREAT HIM, ASTERIX!

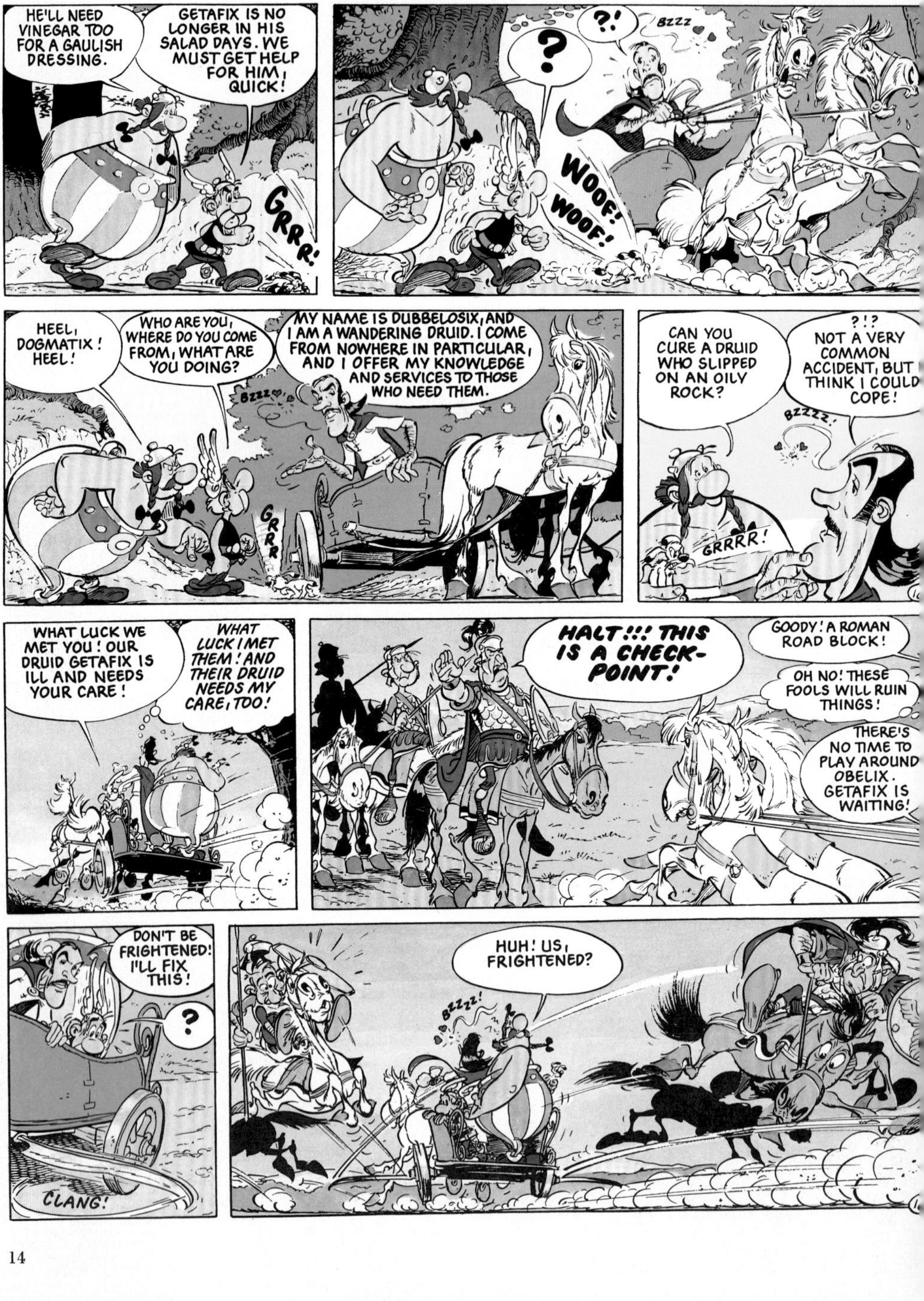
HE'LL NEED VINEGAR TOO FOR A GAULISH DRESSING.
GETAFIX IS NO LONGER IN HIS SALAD DAYS. WE MUST GET HELP FOR HIM, QUICK!
GRRR!
?
?!
BZZZ
WOOF! WOOF!
HEEL, DOGMATIX! HEEL!
WHO ARE YOU, WHERE DO YOU COME FROM, WHAT ARE YOU DOING?
MY NAME IS DUBBELOSIX, AND I AM A WANDERING DRUID. I COME FROM NOWHERE IN PARTICULAR, AND I OFFER MY KNOWLEDGE AND SERVICES TO THOSE WHO NEED THEM.
BZZZ
GRRR
CAN YOU CURE A DRUID WHO SLIPPED ON AN OILY ROCK?
?!? NOT A VERY COMMON ACCIDENT, BUT THINK I COULD COPE!
BZZZZ!
GRRRR!
WHAT LUCK WE MET YOU! OUR DRUID GETAFIX IS ILL AND NEEDS YOUR CARE!
WHAT LUCK I MET THEM! AND THEIR DRUID NEEDS MY CARE, TOO!
HALT!!! THIS IS A CHECK-POINT!
GOODY! A ROMAN ROAD BLOCK!
OH NO! THESE FOOLS WILL RUIN THINGS!
THERE'S NO TIME TO PLAY AROUND OBELIX. GETAFIX IS WAITING!
DON'T BE FRIGHTENED! I'LL FIX THIS!
?
CLANG!
HUH! US, FRIGHTENED?
BZZZZ!

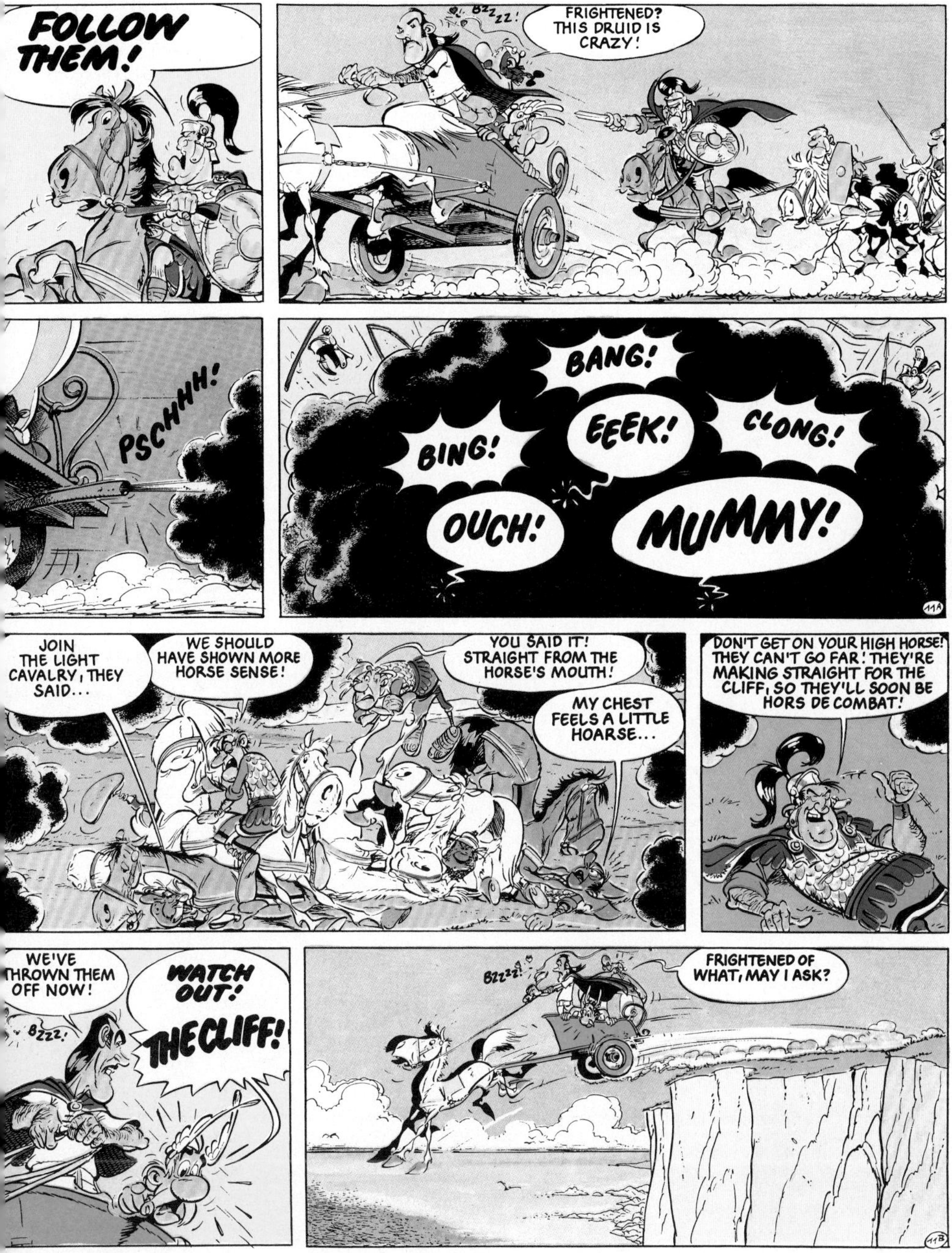
FOLLOW THEM!
BZZZZ!
FRIGHTENED? THIS DRUID IS CRAZY!
PSCHHH!
BANG!
BING!
EEEK!
CLONG!
OUCH!
MUMMY!
JOIN THE LIGHT CAVALRY, THEY SAID...
WE SHOULD HAVE SHOWN MORE HORSE SENSE!
YOU SAID IT! STRAIGHT FROM THE HORSE'S MOUTH!
MY CHEST FEELS A LITTLE HOARSE...
DON'T GET ON YOUR HIGH HORSE! THEY CAN'T GO FAR! THEY'RE MAKING STRAIGHT FOR THE CLIFF, SO THEY'LL SOON BE HORS DE COMBAT!
WE'VE THROWN THEM OFF NOW!
BZZZ!
WATCH OUT! THE CLIFF!
BZZZZ!
FRIGHTENED OF WHAT, MAY I ASK?

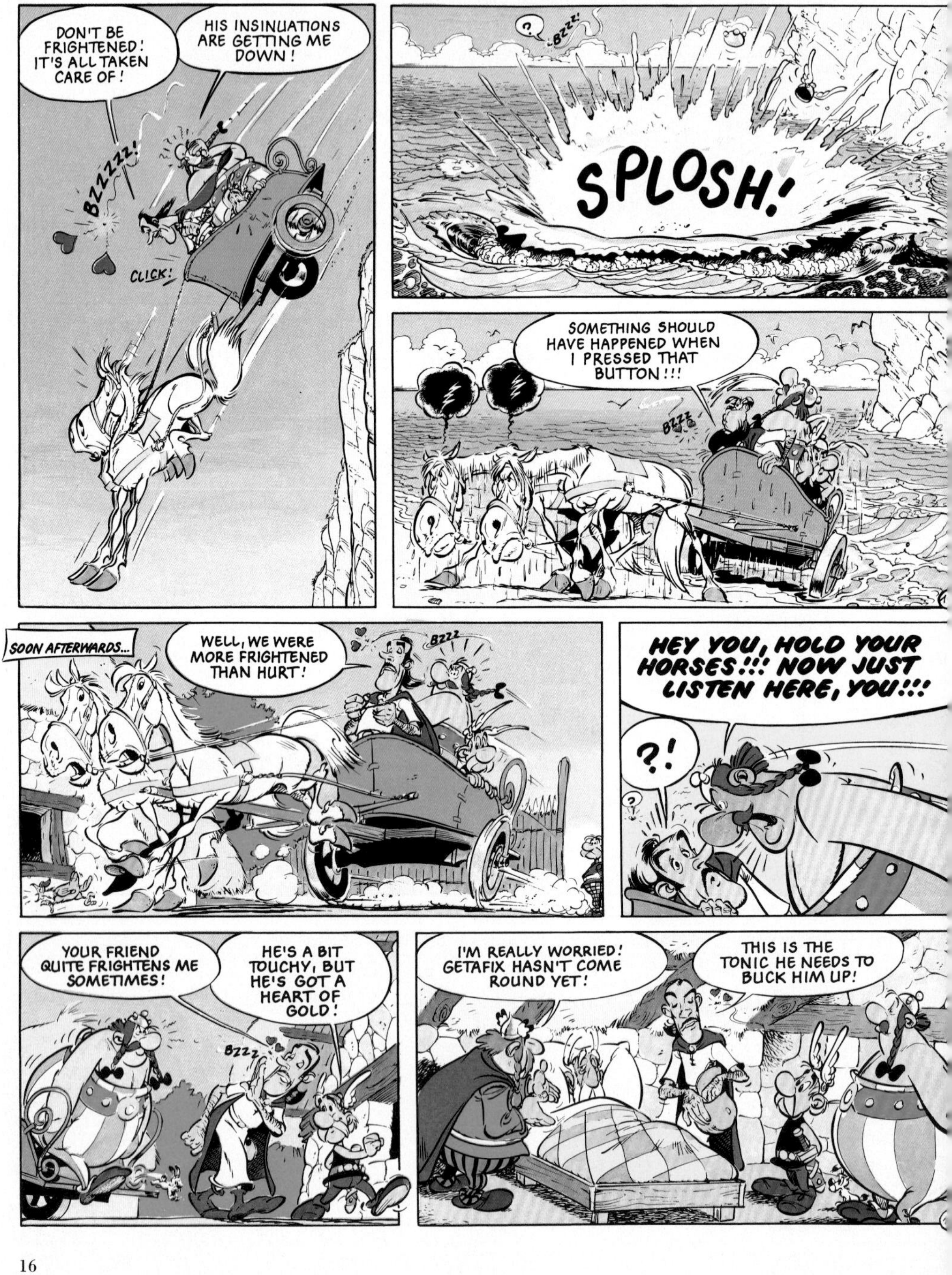
DON'T BE FRIGHTENED! IT'S ALL TAKEN CARE OF!
HIS INSINUATIONS ARE GETTING ME DOWN!
BZZZZZZ!
CLICK!
?
BZZZ!
SPLOSH!
SOMETHING SHOULD HAVE HAPPENED WHEN I PRESSED THAT BUTTON!!!
BZZZ
SOON AFTERWARDS...
WELL, WE WERE MORE FRIGHTENED THAN HURT!
BZZZ
HEY YOU, HOLD YOUR HORSES!!! NOW JUST LISTEN HERE, YOU!!!
?!
?
YOUR FRIEND QUITE FRIGHTENS ME SOMETIMES!
HE'S A BIT TOUCHY, BUT HE'S GOT A HEART OF GOLD!
BZZZ
I'M REALLY WORRIED! GETAFIX HASN'T COME ROUND YET!
THIS IS THE TONIC HE NEEDS TO BUCK HIM UP!

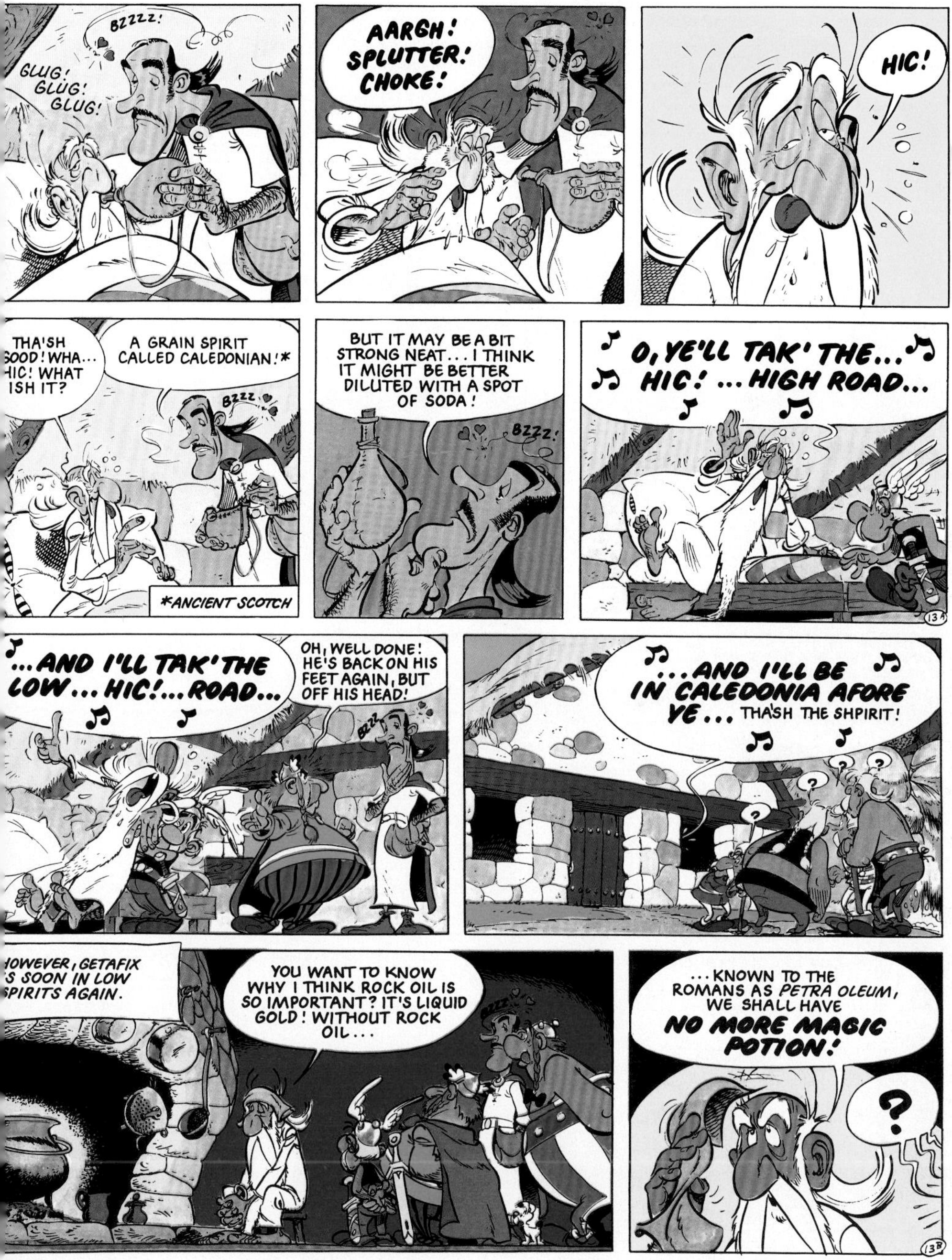
BZZZZ!
GLUG! GLUG! GLUG!
AARGH! SPLUTTER! CHOKE!
HIC!
THA'SH GOOD! WHA... HIC! WHAT ISH IT?
A GRAIN SPIRIT CALLED CALEDONIAN!*
BZZZ
*ANCIENT SCOTCH
BUT IT MAY BE A BIT STRONG NEAT... I THINK IT MIGHT BE BETTER DILUTED WITH A SPOT OF SODA!
BZZZ!
O, YE'LL TAK' THE... HIC! ...HIGH ROAD...
...AND I'LL TAK' THE LOW... HIC!... ROAD...
OH, WELL DONE! HE'S BACK ON HIS FEET AGAIN, BUT OFF HIS HEAD!
BZZZ
...AND I'LL BE IN CALEDONIA AFORE YE... THA'SH THE SHPIRIT!
?
HOWEVER, GETAFIX IS SOON IN LOW SPIRITS AGAIN.
YOU WANT TO KNOW WHY I THINK ROCK OIL IS SO IMPORTANT? IT'S LIQUID GOLD! WITHOUT ROCK OIL...
BZZZ
...KNOWN TO THE ROMANS AS PETRA OLEUM, WE SHALL HAVE NO MORE MAGIC POTION!
?

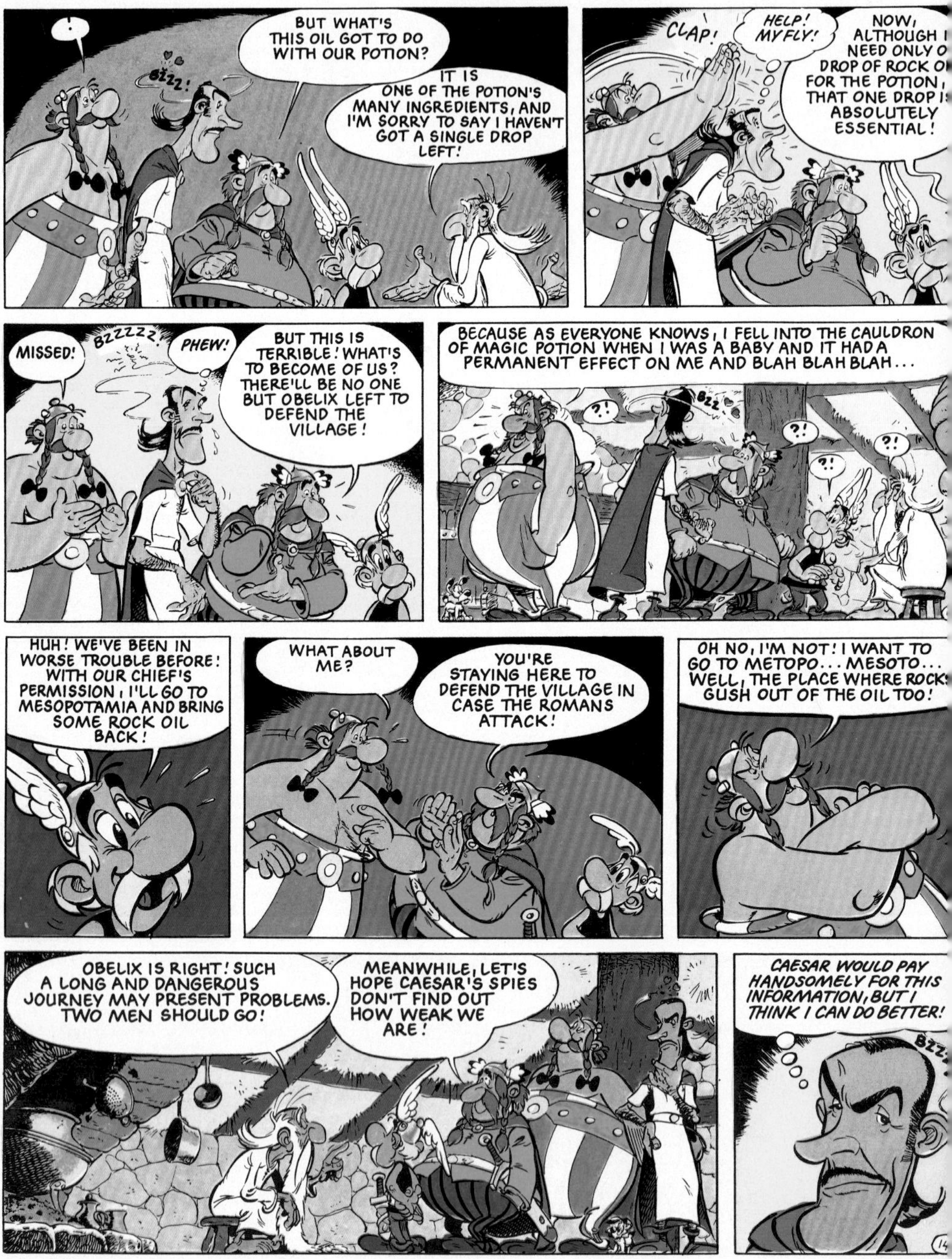
!
BZZZ!
BUT WHAT'S THIS OIL GOT TO DO WITH OUR POTION?
IT IS ONE OF THE POTION'S MANY INGREDIENTS, AND I'M SORRY TO SAY I HAVEN'T GOT A SINGLE DROP LEFT!
CLAP!
HELP! MY FLY!
NOW, ALTHOUGH I NEED ONLY O DROP OF ROCK O FOR THE POTION, THAT ONE DROP I ABSOLUTELY ESSENTIAL!
MISSED!
BZZZZZ!
PHEW!
BUT THIS IS TERRIBLE! WHAT'S TO BECOME OF US? THERE'LL BE NO ONE BUT OBELIX LEFT TO DEFEND THE VILLAGE!
BECAUSE AS EVERYONE KNOWS, I FELL INTO THE CAULDRON OF MAGIC POTION WHEN I WAS A BABY AND IT HAD A PERMANENT EFFECT ON ME AND BLAH BLAH BLAH...
?!
BZZ
?!
?!
?!
HUH! WE'VE BEEN IN WORSE TROUBLE BEFORE! WITH OUR CHIEF'S PERMISSION, I'LL GO TO MESOPOTAMIA AND BRING SOME ROCK OIL BACK!
WHAT ABOUT ME?
YOU'RE STAYING HERE TO DEFEND THE VILLAGE IN CASE THE ROMANS ATTACK!
OH NO, I'M NOT! I WANT TO GO TO METOPO... MESOTO... WELL, THE PLACE WHERE ROCKS GUSH OUT OF THE OIL TOO!
OBELIX IS RIGHT! SUCH A LONG AND DANGEROUS JOURNEY MAY PRESENT PROBLEMS. TWO MEN SHOULD GO!
MEANWHILE, LET'S HOPE CAESAR'S SPIES DON'T FIND OUT HOW WEAK WE ARE!
CAESAR WOULD PAY HANDSOMELY FOR THIS INFORMATION, BUT I THINK I CAN DO BETTER!
BZZ

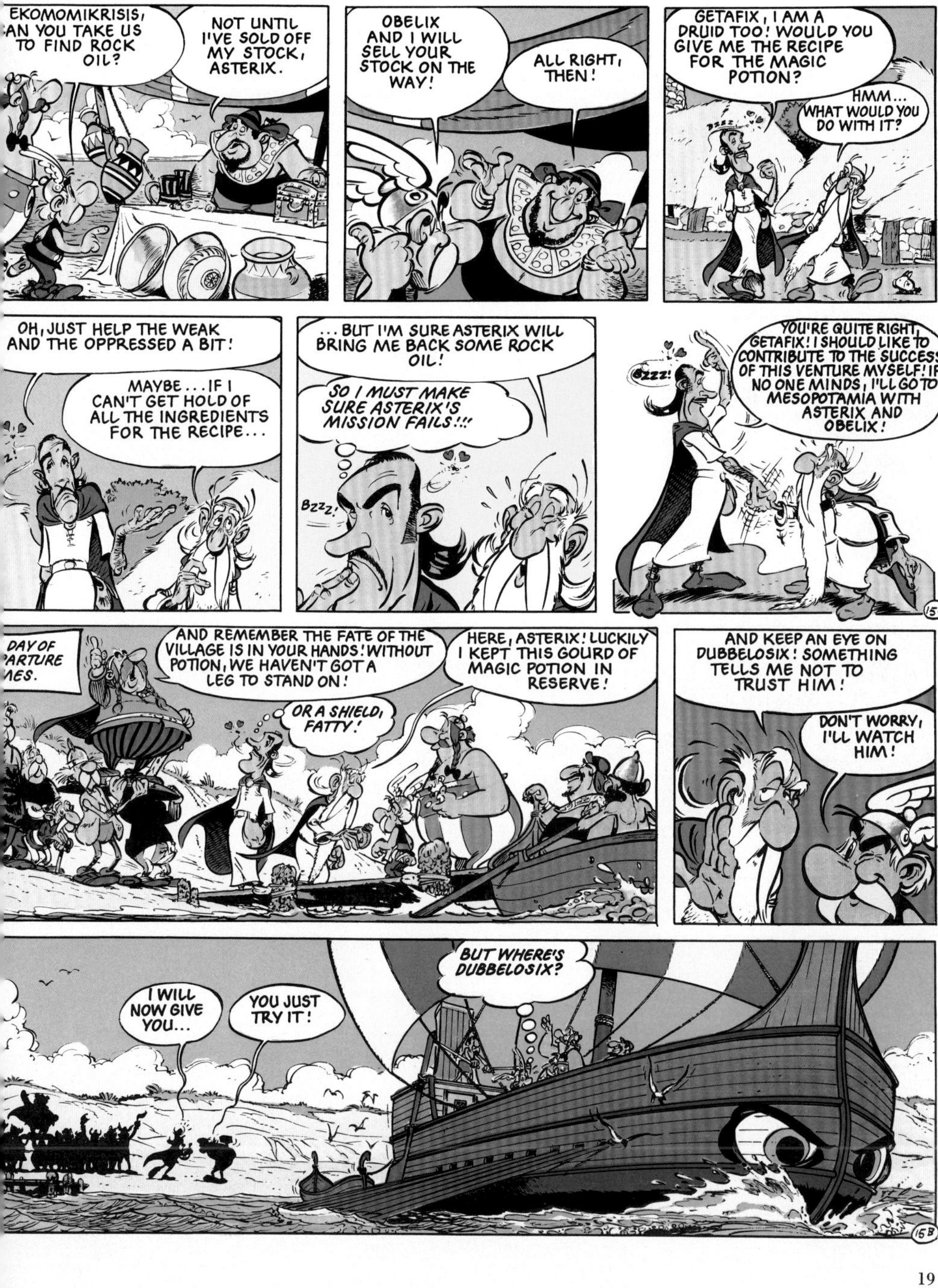
EKOMOMIKRISIS, AN YOU TAKE US TO FIND ROCK OIL?
NOT UNTIL I'VE SOLD OFF MY STOCK, ASTERIX.
OBELIX AND I WILL SELL YOUR STOCK ON THE WAY!
ALL RIGHT, THEN!
GETAFIX, I AM A DRUID TOO! WOULD YOU GIVE ME THE RECIPE FOR THE MAGIC POTION?
BZZZ
HMM... WHAT WOULD YOU DO WITH IT?
OH, JUST HELP THE WEAK AND THE OPPRESSED A BIT!
MAYBE... IF I CAN'T GET HOLD OF ALL THE INGREDIENTS FOR THE RECIPE...
... BUT I'M SURE ASTERIX WILL BRING ME BACK SOME ROCK OIL!
SO I MUST MAKE SURE ASTERIX'S MISSION FAILS!!!
BZZZ!
BZZZ!
YOU'RE QUITE RIGHT, GETAFIX! I SHOULD LIKE TO CONTRIBUTE TO THE SUCCESS OF THIS VENTURE MYSELF! IF NO ONE MINDS, I'LL GO TO MESOPOTAMIA WITH ASTERIX AND OBELIX!
15A
DAY OF PARTURE MES.
AND REMEMBER THE FATE OF THE VILLAGE IS IN YOUR HANDS! WITHOUT POTION, WE HAVEN'T GOT A LEG TO STAND ON!
OR A SHIELD, FATTY!
HERE, ASTERIX! LUCKILY I KEPT THIS GOURD OF MAGIC POTION IN RESERVE!
AND KEEP AN EYE ON DUBBELOSIX! SOMETHING TELLS ME NOT TO TRUST HIM!
DON'T WORRY, I'LL WATCH HIM!
I WILL NOW GIVE YOU...
YOU JUST TRY IT!
BUT WHERE'S DUBBELOSIX?
15B

NOW, TAKE MY MESSAGE TO SURREPTITIUS!

NO DAWDLING ON THE WAY! IT'S URGENT!

BZZZZ

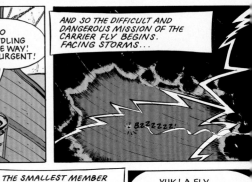

AND SO THE DIFFICULT AND DANGEROUS MISSION OF THE CARRIER FLY BEGINS. FACING STORMS...

BZZZZZZ

...AND MANY OTHER PERILS...

?!

BZZZZZ

ZIP!
ZIP!
ZIP!
ZIP!
SNAP!

...THE SMALLEST MEMBER OF CAESAR'S SECRET SERVICE FINALLY REACHES HER JOURNEY'S END, WORN OUT.

BZZZZZZZZ

?!

FLOP!

YUK! A FLY IN MY SOUP!! HOW REVOLTING!!!

EUGGH!

WHY WAS I IN THE SOUP? WHAT'S BUGGING HIM?

PLOP!

LET'S SEE WHAT DUBBELOSIX HAS TO SAY. "AM ON PHOENICIAN SHIP BOUND FOR MESOPOTAMIA, WITH INDOMITABLE GAULS. AT ALL COSTS PREVENT LANDING."

WELL, DUBBELOSIX MUST HAVE HIS REASONS. I'LL GO AND GIVE THE NECESSARY ORDERS!

AND YOU FLY STRAIGHT BACK TO DUBBELOSIX! SHOO!

TAKE IT EASY! YOU MAY FIND I'M A FLY IN THE OINTMENT!

MEANWHILE, SAILING THE HIGH SEAS...

IT'S A FUNNY THING, ASTERIX, DUBBELOSIX HASN'T BEEN ATTRACTING INSECTS LATELY!

NO, I FANCY THERE ARE NO FLIES ON HIM!

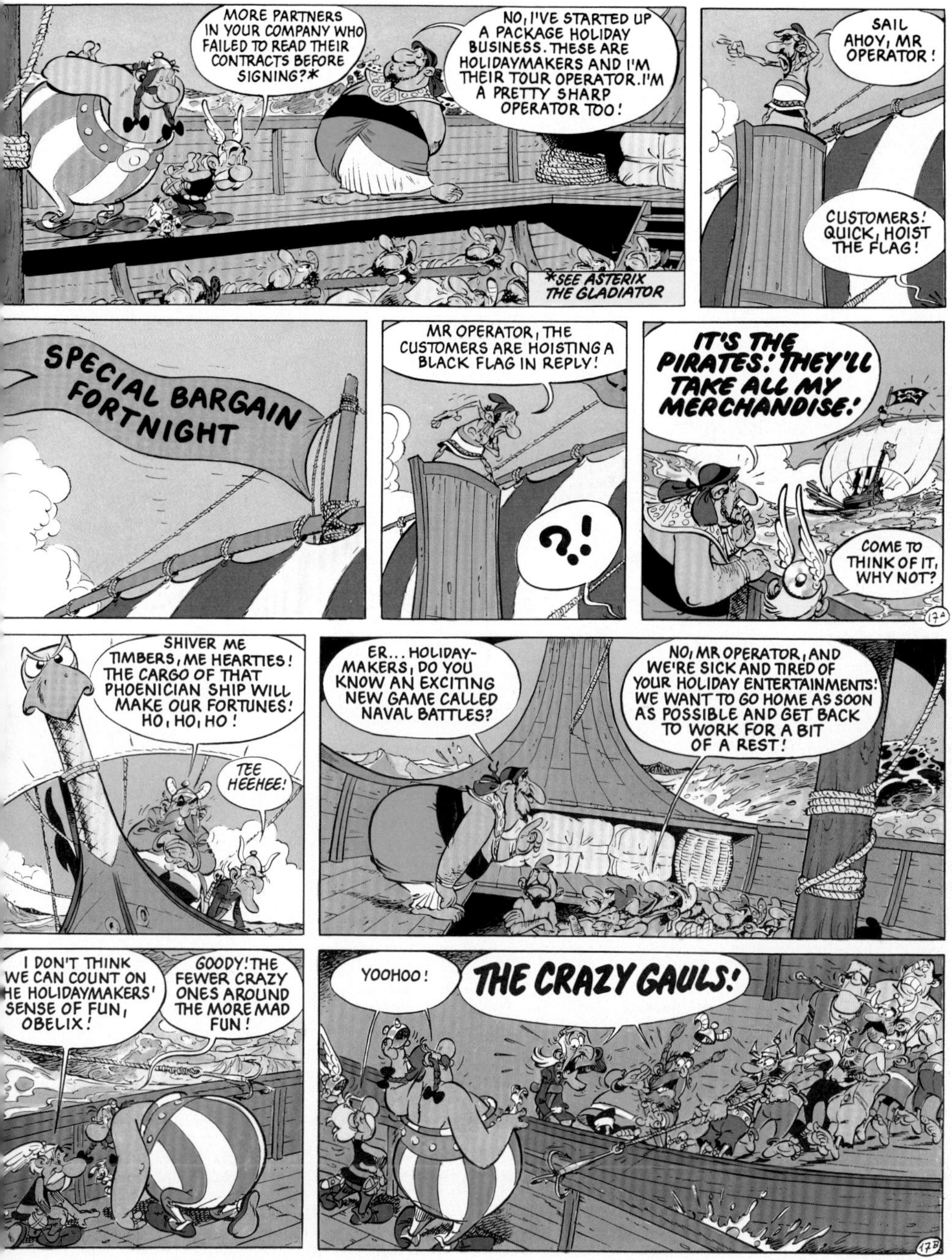
MORE PARTNERS IN YOUR COMPANY WHO FAILED TO READ THEIR CONTRACTS BEFORE SIGNING?*
NO, I'VE STARTED UP A PACKAGE HOLIDAY BUSINESS. THESE ARE HOLIDAYMAKERS AND I'M THEIR TOUR OPERATOR. I'M A PRETTY SHARP OPERATOR TOO!
*SEE ASTERIX THE GLADIATOR
SAIL AHOY, MR OPERATOR!
CUSTOMERS! QUICK, HOIST THE FLAG!
SPECIAL BARGAIN FORTNIGHT
MR OPERATOR, THE CUSTOMERS ARE HOISTING A BLACK FLAG IN REPLY!
?!
IT'S THE PIRATES! THEY'LL TAKE ALL MY MERCHANDISE!
COME TO THINK OF IT, WHY NOT?
17A
SHIVER ME TIMBERS, ME HEARTIES! THE CARGO OF THAT PHOENICIAN SHIP WILL MAKE OUR FORTUNES! HO, HO, HO!
TEE HEEHEE!
ER... HOLIDAY-MAKERS, DO YOU KNOW AN EXCITING NEW GAME CALLED NAVAL BATTLES?
NO, MR OPERATOR, AND WE'RE SICK AND TIRED OF YOUR HOLIDAY ENTERTAINMENTS! WE WANT TO GO HOME AS SOON AS POSSIBLE AND GET BACK TO WORK FOR A BIT OF A REST!
I DON'T THINK WE CAN COUNT ON HE HOLIDAYMAKERS' SENSE OF FUN, OBELIX!
GOODY! THE FEWER CRAZY ONES AROUND THE MORE MAD FUN!
YOOHOO!
THE CRAZY GAULS!
17B

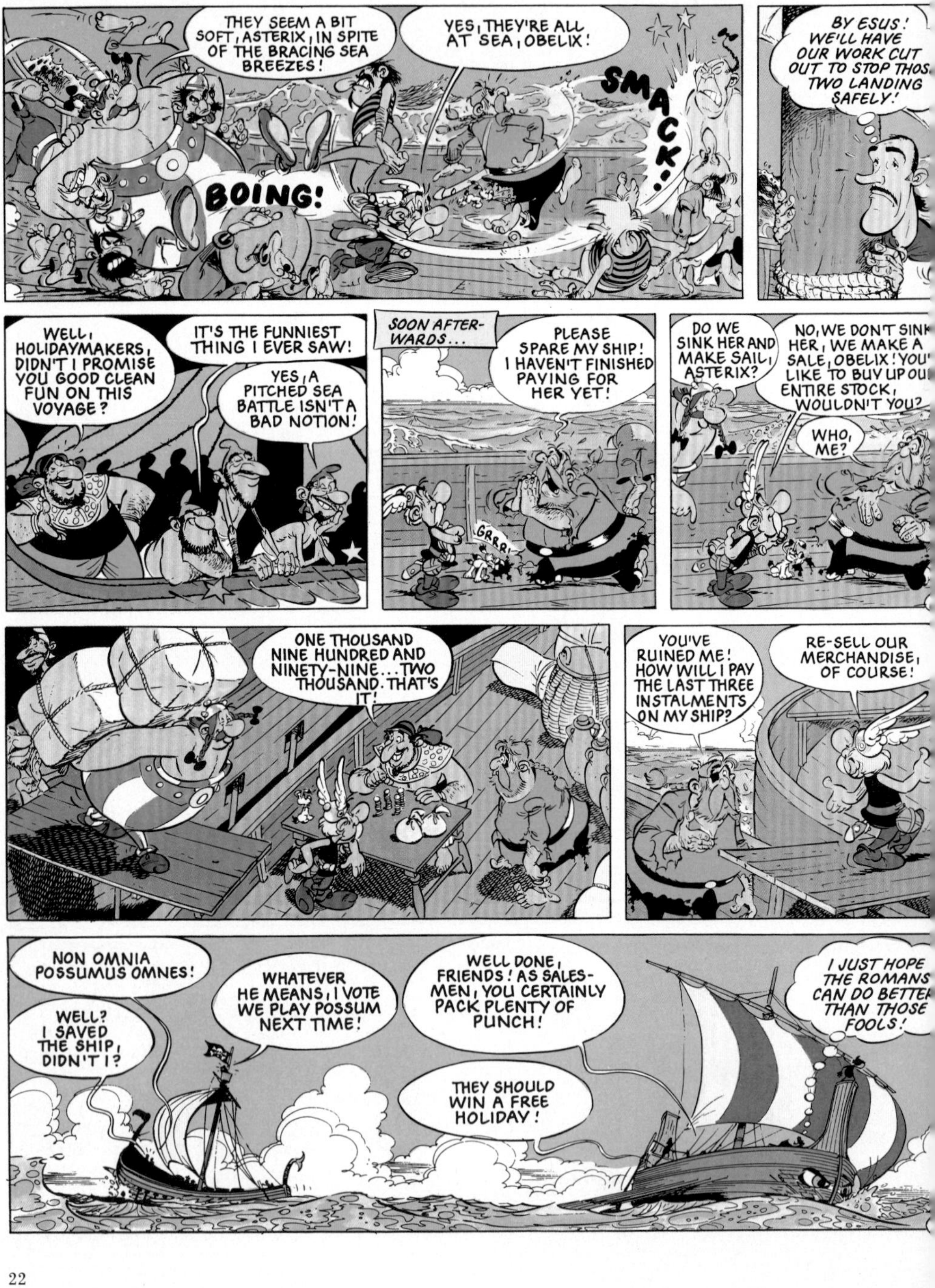
THEY SEEM A BIT SOFT, ASTERIX, IN SPITE OF THE BRACING SEA BREEZES!
YES, THEY'RE ALL AT SEA, OBELIX!
BOING!
SMACK!
BY ESUS! WE'LL HAVE OUR WORK CUT OUT TO STOP THOS TWO LANDING SAFELY!
WELL, HOLIDAYMAKERS, DIDN'T I PROMISE YOU GOOD CLEAN FUN ON THIS VOYAGE?
IT'S THE FUNNIEST THING I EVER SAW!
YES, A PITCHED SEA BATTLE ISN'T A BAD NOTION!
SOON AFTERWARDS...
PLEASE SPARE MY SHIP! I HAVEN'T FINISHED PAYING FOR HER YET!
GRRR!
DO WE SINK HER AND MAKE SAIL, ASTERIX?
NO, WE DON'T SINK HER, WE MAKE A SALE, OBELIX! YOU' LIKE TO BUY UP OU ENTIRE STOCK, WOULDN'T YOU?
WHO, ME?
ONE THOUSAND NINE HUNDRED AND NINETY-NINE... TWO THOUSAND. THAT'S IT!
YOU'VE RUINED ME! HOW WILL I PAY THE LAST THREE INSTALMENTS ON MY SHIP?
RE-SELL OUR MERCHANDISE, OF COURSE!
NON OMNIA POSSUMUS OMNES!
WELL? I SAVED THE SHIP, DIDN'T I?
WHATEVER HE MEANS, I VOTE WE PLAY POSSUM NEXT TIME!
WELL DONE, FRIENDS! AS SALESMEN, YOU CERTAINLY PACK PLENTY OF PUNCH!
THEY SHOULD WIN A FREE HOLIDAY!
I JUST HOPE THE ROMANS CAN DO BETTE THAN THOSE FOOLS!

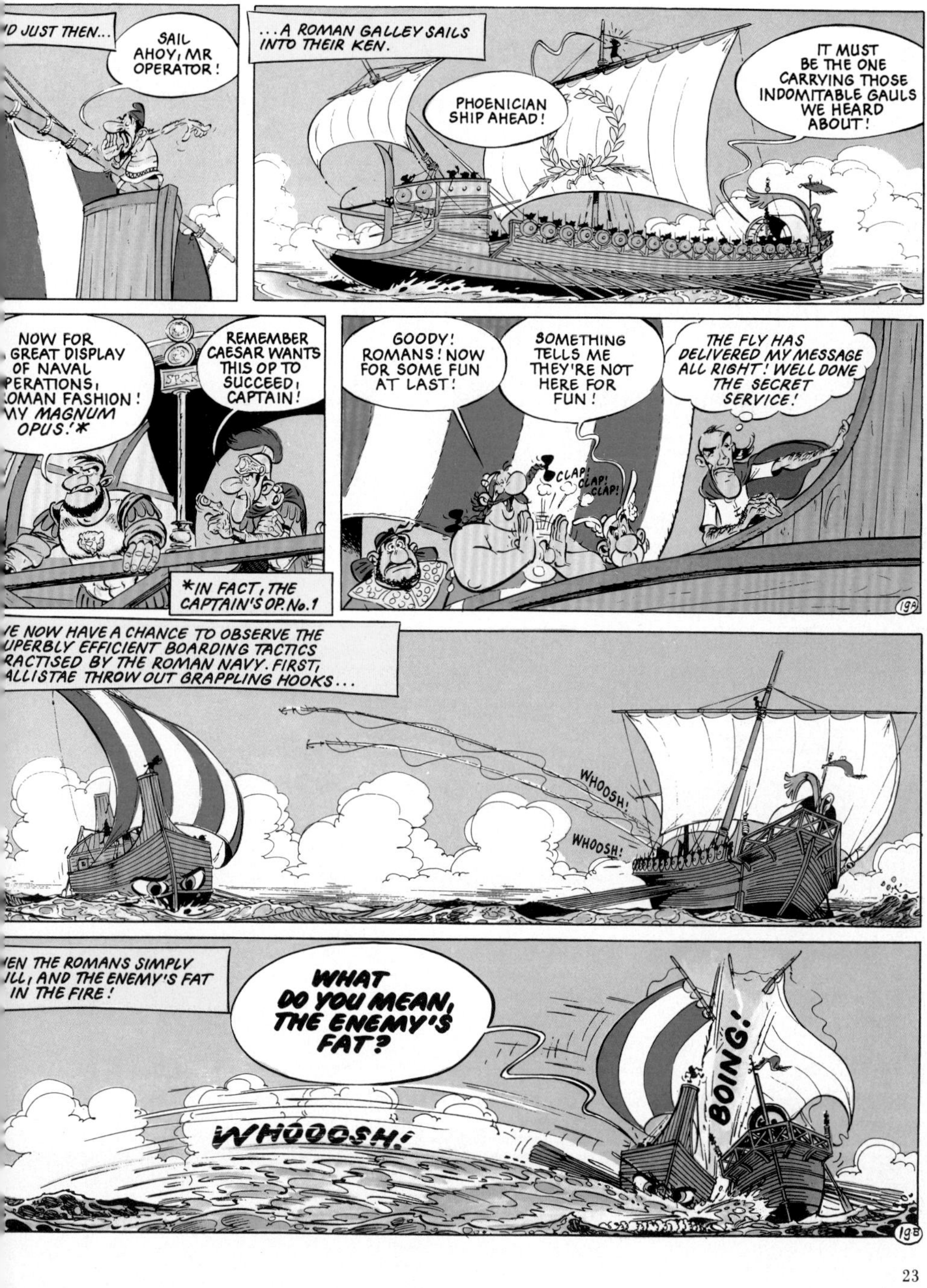
D JUST THEN...
SAIL AHOY, MR OPERATOR!
...A ROMAN GALLEY SAILS INTO THEIR KEN.
PHOENICIAN SHIP AHEAD!
IT MUST BE THE ONE CARRYING THOSE INDOMITABLE GAULS WE HEARD ABOUT!
NOW FOR GREAT DISPLAY OF NAVAL PERATIONS, ROMAN FASHION! MY MAGNUM OPUS!*
REMEMBER CAESAR WANTS THIS OP TO SUCCEED, CAPTAIN!
*IN FACT, THE CAPTAIN'S OP. No. 1
GOODY! ROMANS! NOW FOR SOME FUN AT LAST!
SOMETHING TELLS ME THEY'RE NOT HERE FOR FUN!
CLAP! CLAP! CLAP!
THE FLY HAS DELIVERED MY MESSAGE ALL RIGHT! WELL DONE THE SECRET SERVICE!
19A
VE NOW HAVE A CHANCE TO OBSERVE THE UPERBLY EFFICIENT BOARDING TACTICS RACTISED BY THE ROMAN NAVY. FIRST, ALLISTAE THROW OUT GRAPPLING HOOKS...
WHOOSH!
WHOOSH!
IEN THE ROMANS SIMPLY ILL, AND THE ENEMY'S FAT IN THE FIRE!
WHAT DO YOU MEAN, THE ENEMY'S FAT?
BOING!
WHOOOOSH!
19B

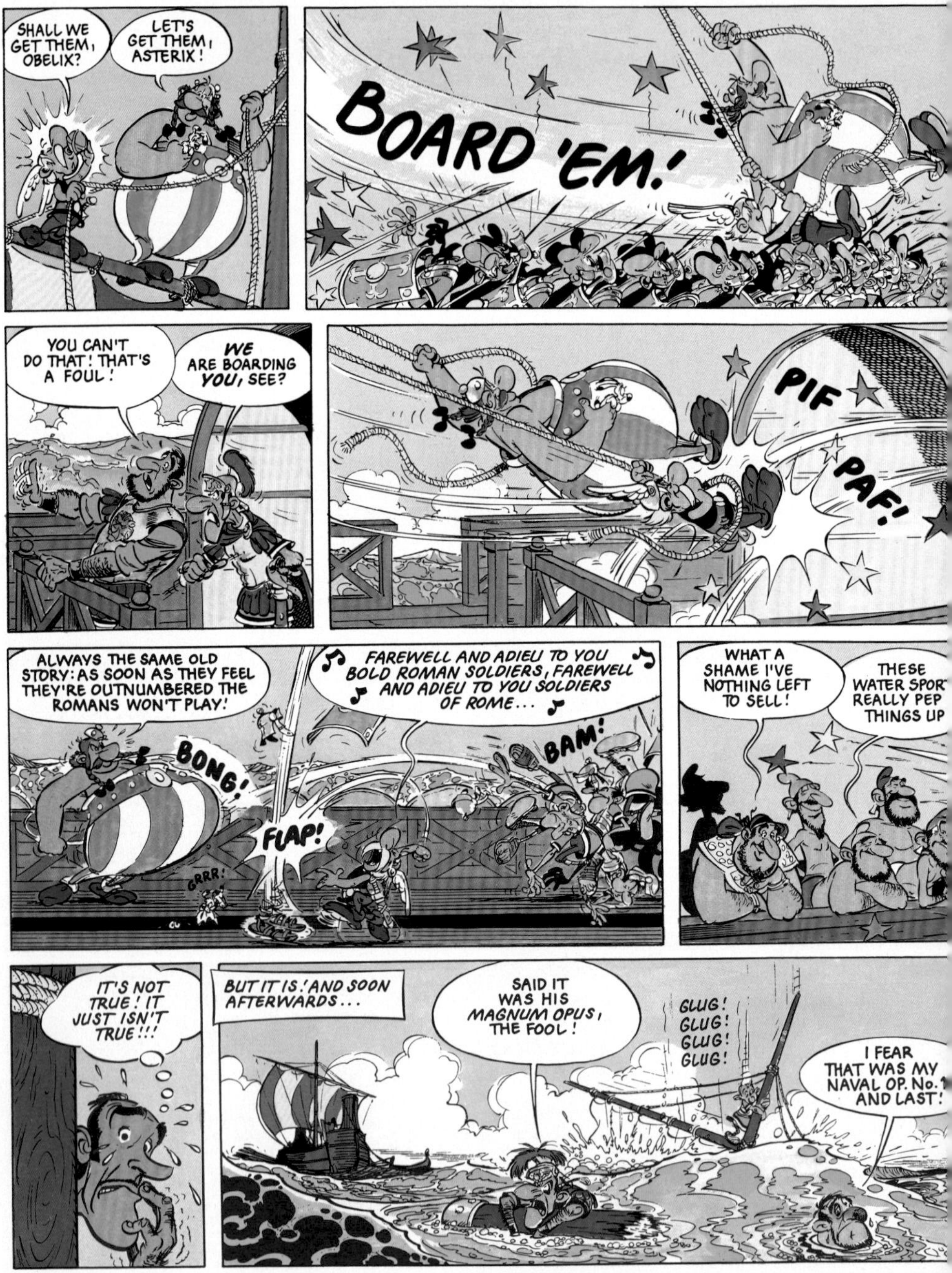

SHALL WE GET THEM, OBELIX?
LET'S GET THEM, ASTERIX!
BOARD 'EM!
YOU CAN'T DO THAT! THAT'S A FOUL!
WE ARE BOARDING YOU, SEE?
PIF
PAF!
ALWAYS THE SAME OLD STORY: AS SOON AS THEY FEEL THEY'RE OUTNUMBERED THE ROMANS WON'T PLAY!
FAREWELL AND ADIEU TO YOU BOLD ROMAN SOLDIERS, FAREWELL AND ADIEU TO YOU SOLDIERS OF ROME...
BONG!
BAM!
FLAP!
GRRR!
WHAT A SHAME I'VE NOTHING LEFT TO SELL!
THESE WATER SPORT REALLY PEP THINGS UP
IT'S NOT TRUE! IT JUST ISN'T TRUE!!!
BUT IT IS! AND SOON AFTERWARDS...
SAID IT WAS HIS MAGNUM OPUS, THE FOOL!
GLUG! GLUG! GLUG! GLUG!
I FEAR THAT WAS MY NAVAL OP. No. 1 AND LAST!

...ND ONCE
...AIN...

ROMAN
GALLEY
AHOY, MR
OPERATOR.

...THE NOW CLASSIC BOARDING TACTICS...

BONG!

...ARE FOLLOWED BY AN EQUALLY ADITIONAL FIGHT AND ITS AFTERMATH.

WE'RE HAVING FUN, AREN'T WE, ASTERIX?

BANG!

BING!

BIFF!

PAF!

YES, BUT IT SEEMS ODD FOR THE ROMANS TO BE SO KEEN ON FIGHTING US, OBELIX!

EVERY TIME I SEE IT AGAIN I FIND SOMETHING ELSE TO APPRECIATE!

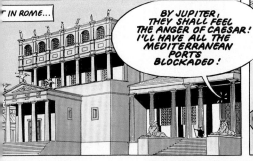

IN ROME...

BY JUPITER, THEY SHALL FEEL THE ANGER OF CAESAR! I'LL HAVE ALL THE MEDITERRANEAN PORTS BLOCKADED!

AND LOOK SHARP! I DON'T EXPECT MY NAVAL COMMANDERS TO STOP AND CONTEMPLATE ANY NAVELS!*

*POPULAR MEDITERRANEAN FRUIT

I WANT TO MAKE SURE NOT EVEN A FLY COULD GET THROUGH THE NET!

HM...AND THINKING OF FLIES...

SURREPTITIUS!

ANY NEWS OF YOUR AGENT DUBBEL...DUBBEL SOMETHING?

I'M AFRAID WE HAVE A COMMUNICATIONS PROBLEM, O CAESAR!

SNAP!

PROBLEM? WHAT SORT OF PROBLEM?

OUR CARRIER FLY IS GOING SLOW, AND IF SHE ACTUALLY GOES ON STRIKE...

WELL, IF IT'S WILDLIFE WE'RE DISCUSSING, HOW WOULD YOU LIKE TO FIND OUT IF THE LIONS IN THE CIRCUS ARE ON HUNGER STRIKE?!!!

BONK!

I MUST TRY TO ENTICE HER BACK...

WHERE'S A PRETTY FLY, THEN..?

HONEY

BZZ ZZ ZZZZZZZZZZZZZ

BZZZZ ZZZZZ

I MIGHT HAVE KNOWN IT!

HONEY

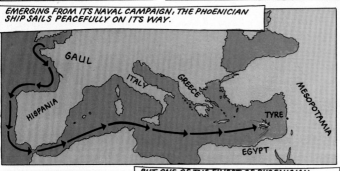

EMERGING FROM ITS NAVAL CAMPAIGN, THE PHOENICIAN SHIP SAILS PEACEFULLY ON ITS WAY.

GAUL

HISPANIA

ITALY

GREECE

MESOPOTAMIA

TYRE

EGYPT

ASTERIX, I'M TIRED OF THIS VOYAGE, AND I GET HUNGRY WHEN I'M TIRED!

WAIT A BIT LONGER OBELIX. WE SHOULD SOON BE LANDING AT TYRE!

DON'T TIRE NOW, HERE COMES TYRE!

BUT ONE OF THE FINEST OF PHOENICIAN TRADING PORTS HAS BECOME INACCESSIBLE. THE HARBOUR MOUTH IS BLOCKED BY BIREMES, TRIREMES, QUADRIREMES AND QUINQUIREMES.

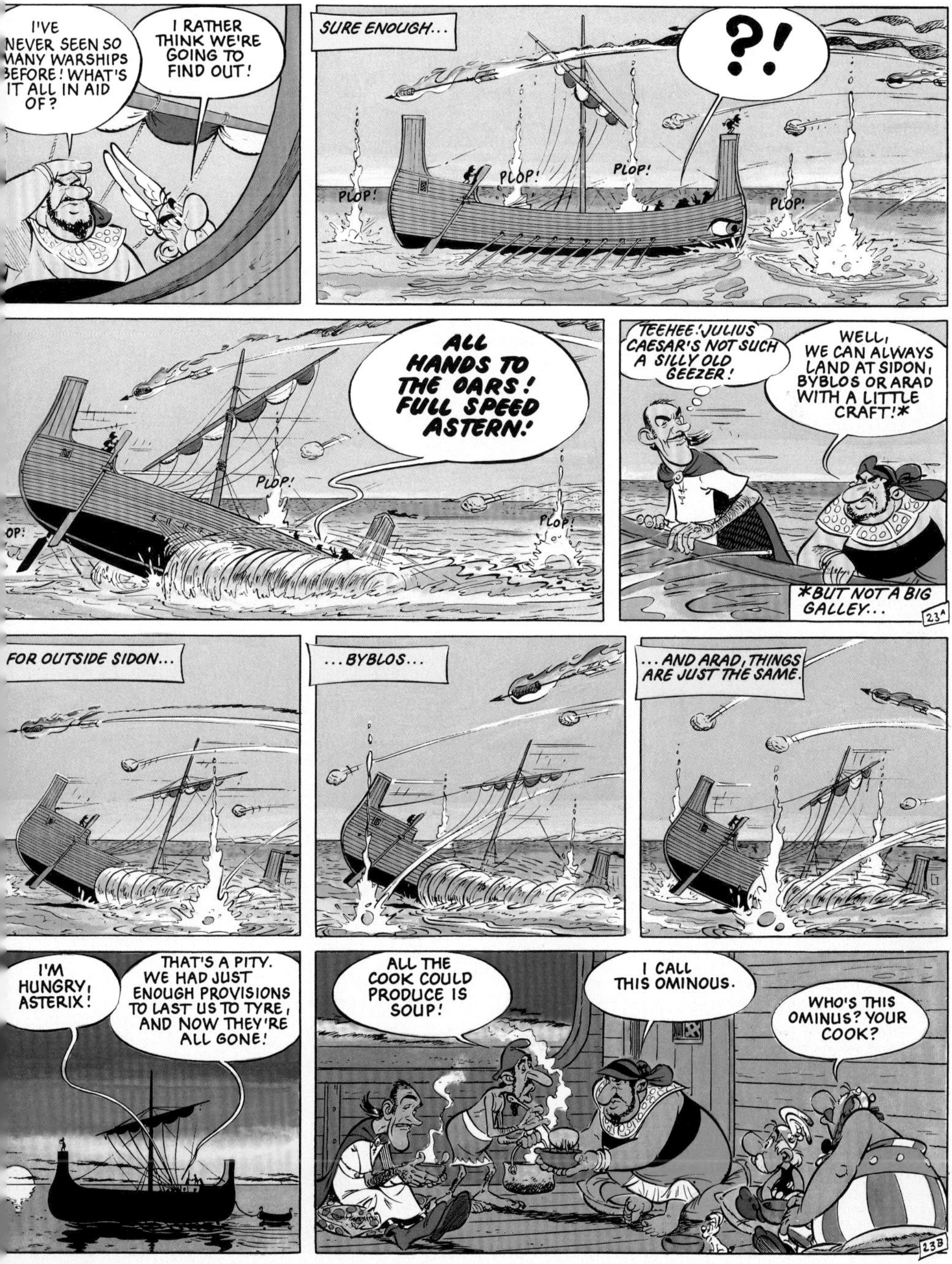
I'VE NEVER SEEN SO MANY WARSHIPS BEFORE! WHAT'S IT ALL IN AID OF?
I RATHER THINK WE'RE GOING TO FIND OUT!
SURE ENOUGH...
?!
PLOP!
PLOP!
PLOP!
PLOP!
ALL HANDS TO THE OARS! FULL SPEED ASTERN!
PLOP!
PLOP!
TEEHEE! JULIUS CAESAR'S NOT SUCH A SILLY OLD GEEZER!
WELL, WE CAN ALWAYS LAND AT SIDON, BYBLOS OR ARAD WITH A LITTLE CRAFT!*
*BUT NOT A BIG GALLEY...
FOR OUTSIDE SIDON...
...BYBLOS...
...AND ARAD, THINGS ARE JUST THE SAME.
I'M HUNGRY, ASTERIX!
THAT'S A PITY. WE HAD JUST ENOUGH PROVISIONS TO LAST US TO TYRE, AND NOW THEY'RE ALL GONE!
ALL THE COOK COULD PRODUCE IS SOUP!
I CALL THIS OMINOUS.
WHO'S THIS OMINUS? YOUR COOK?

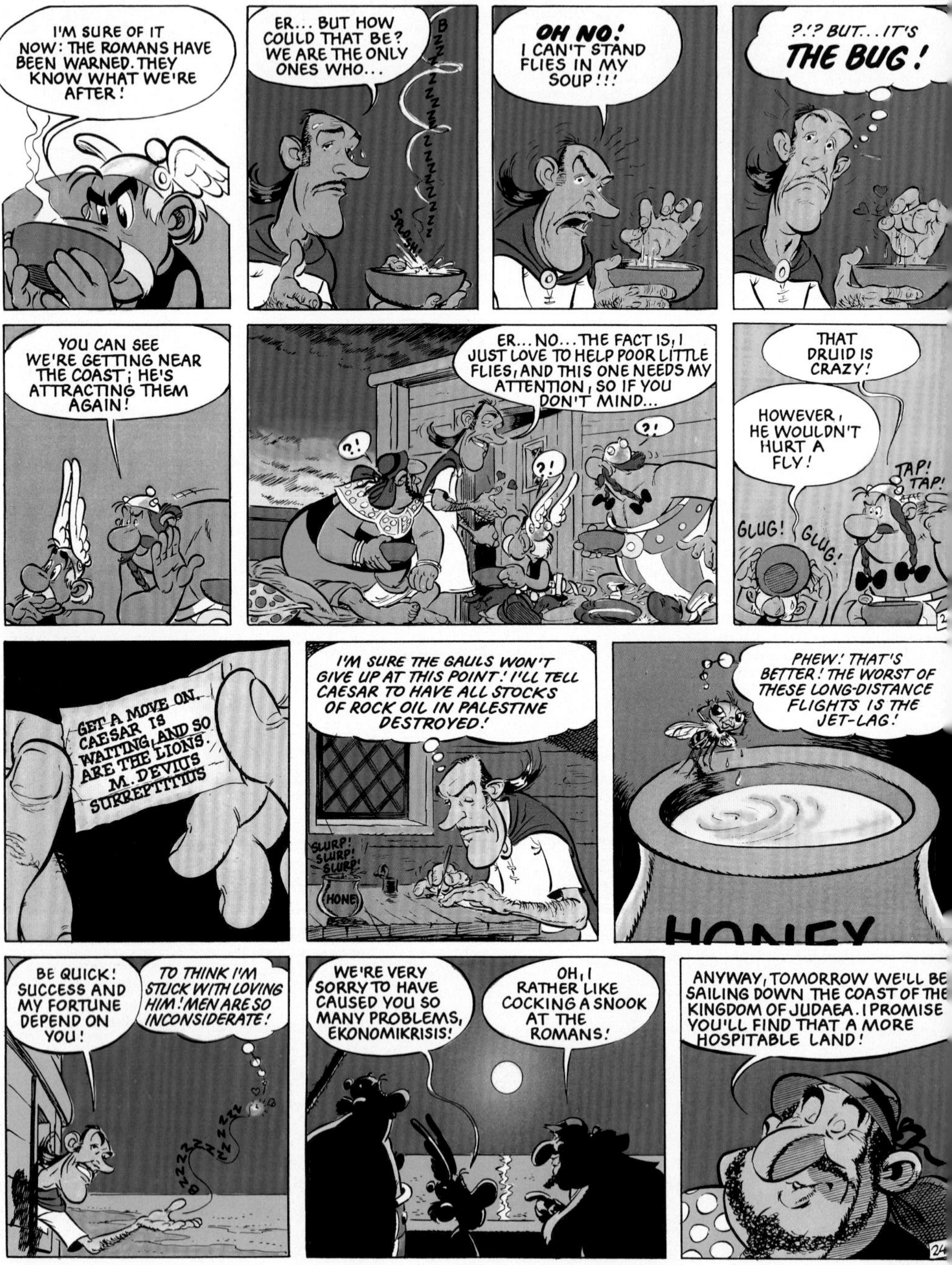
I'M SURE OF IT NOW: THE ROMANS HAVE BEEN WARNED. THEY KNOW WHAT WE'RE AFTER!
ER... BUT HOW COULD THAT BE? WE ARE THE ONLY ONES WHO...
SPLOSH!
OH NO! I CAN'T STAND FLIES IN MY SOUP!!!
?!? BUT... IT'S THE BUG!
YOU CAN SEE WE'RE GETTING NEAR THE COAST; HE'S ATTRACTING THEM AGAIN!
ER... NO... THE FACT IS, I JUST LOVE TO HELP POOR LITTLE FLIES, AND THIS ONE NEEDS MY ATTENTION, SO IF YOU DON'T MIND...
?!
?!
?!
THAT DRUID IS CRAZY!
HOWEVER, HE WOULDN'T HURT A FLY!
TAP! TAP!
GLUG! GLUG!
GET A MOVE ON. CAESAR IS WAITING, AND SO ARE THE LIONS. M. DEVIUS SURREPTITIUS
I'M SURE THE GAULS WON'T GIVE UP AT THIS POINT! I'LL TELL CAESAR TO HAVE ALL STOCKS OF ROCK OIL IN PALESTINE DESTROYED!
SLURP! SLURP! SLURP!
HONE
PHEW! THAT'S BETTER! THE WORST OF THESE LONG-DISTANCE FLIGHTS IS THE JET-LAG!
HONEY
BE QUICK! SUCCESS AND MY FORTUNE DEPEND ON YOU!
TO THINK I'M STUCK WITH LOVING HIM! MEN ARE SO INCONSIDERATE!
WE'RE VERY SORRY TO HAVE CAUSED YOU SO MANY PROBLEMS, EKONOMIKRISIS!
OH, I RATHER LIKE COCKING A SNOOK AT THE ROMANS!
ANYWAY, TOMORROW WE'LL BE SAILING DOWN THE COAST OF THE KINGDOM OF JUDAEA. I PROMISE YOU'LL FIND THAT A MORE HOSPITABLE LAND!
24

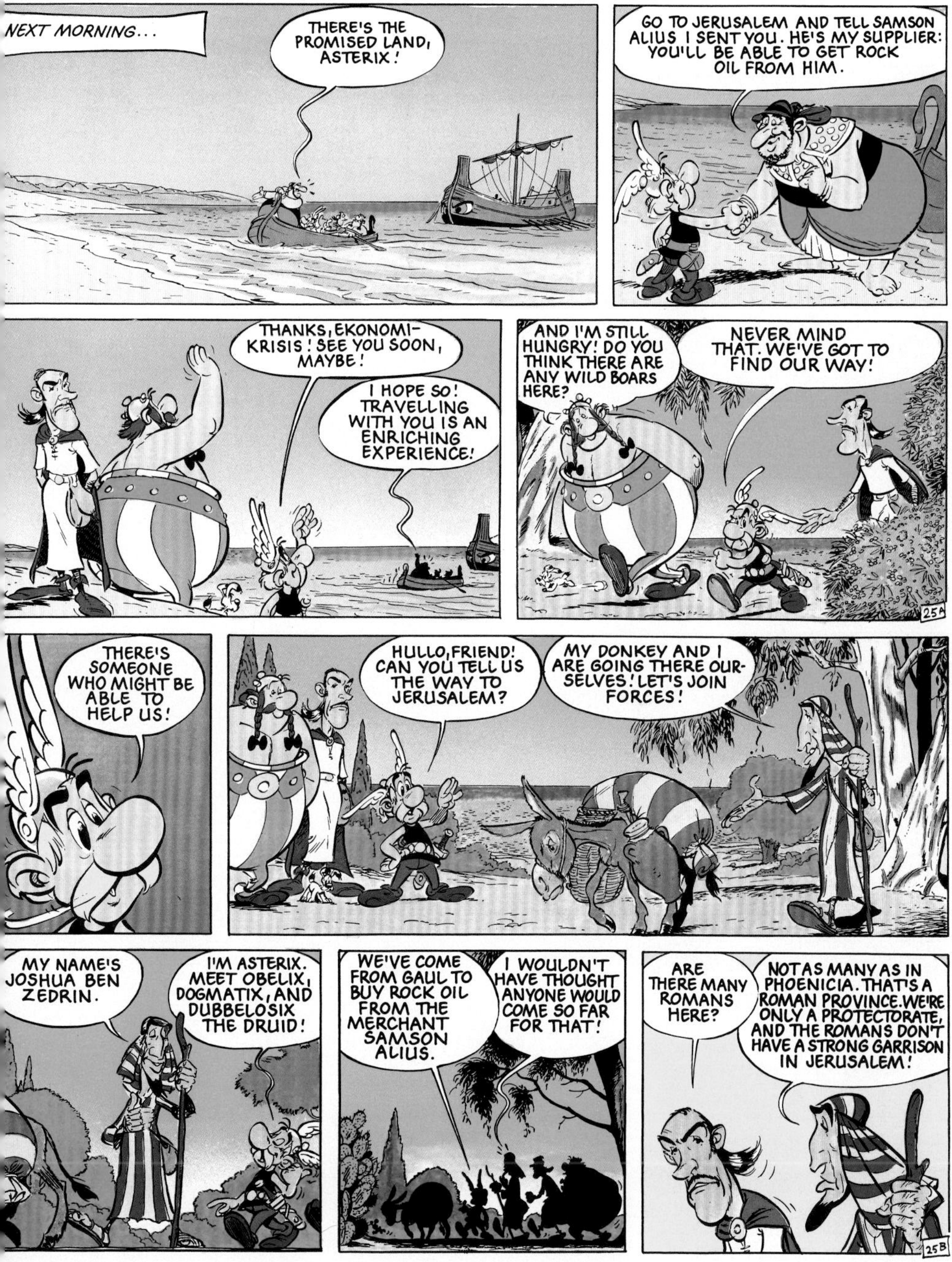
NEXT MORNING...
THERE'S THE PROMISED LAND, ASTERIX!
GO TO JERUSALEM AND TELL SAMSON ALIUS I SENT YOU. HE'S MY SUPPLIER: YOU'LL BE ABLE TO GET ROCK OIL FROM HIM.
THANKS, EKONOMIKRISIS! SEE YOU SOON, MAYBE!
I HOPE SO! TRAVELLING WITH YOU IS AN ENRICHING EXPERIENCE!
AND I'M STILL HUNGRY! DO YOU THINK THERE ARE ANY WILD BOARS HERE?
NEVER MIND THAT. WE'VE GOT TO FIND OUR WAY!
25A
THERE'S SOMEONE WHO MIGHT BE ABLE TO HELP US!
HULLO, FRIEND! CAN YOU TELL US THE WAY TO JERUSALEM?
MY DONKEY AND I ARE GOING THERE OURSELVES! LET'S JOIN FORCES!
MY NAME'S JOSHUA BEN ZEDRIN.
I'M ASTERIX. MEET OBELIX, DOGMATIX, AND DUBBELOSIX THE DRUID!
WE'VE COME FROM GAUL TO BUY ROCK OIL FROM THE MERCHANT SAMSON ALIUS.
I WOULDN'T HAVE THOUGHT ANYONE WOULD COME SO FAR FOR THAT!
ARE THERE MANY ROMANS HERE?
NOT AS MANY AS IN PHOENICIA. THAT'S A ROMAN PROVINCE. WE'RE ONLY A PROTECTORATE, AND THE ROMANS DON'T HAVE A STRONG GARRISON IN JERUSALEM!
25B

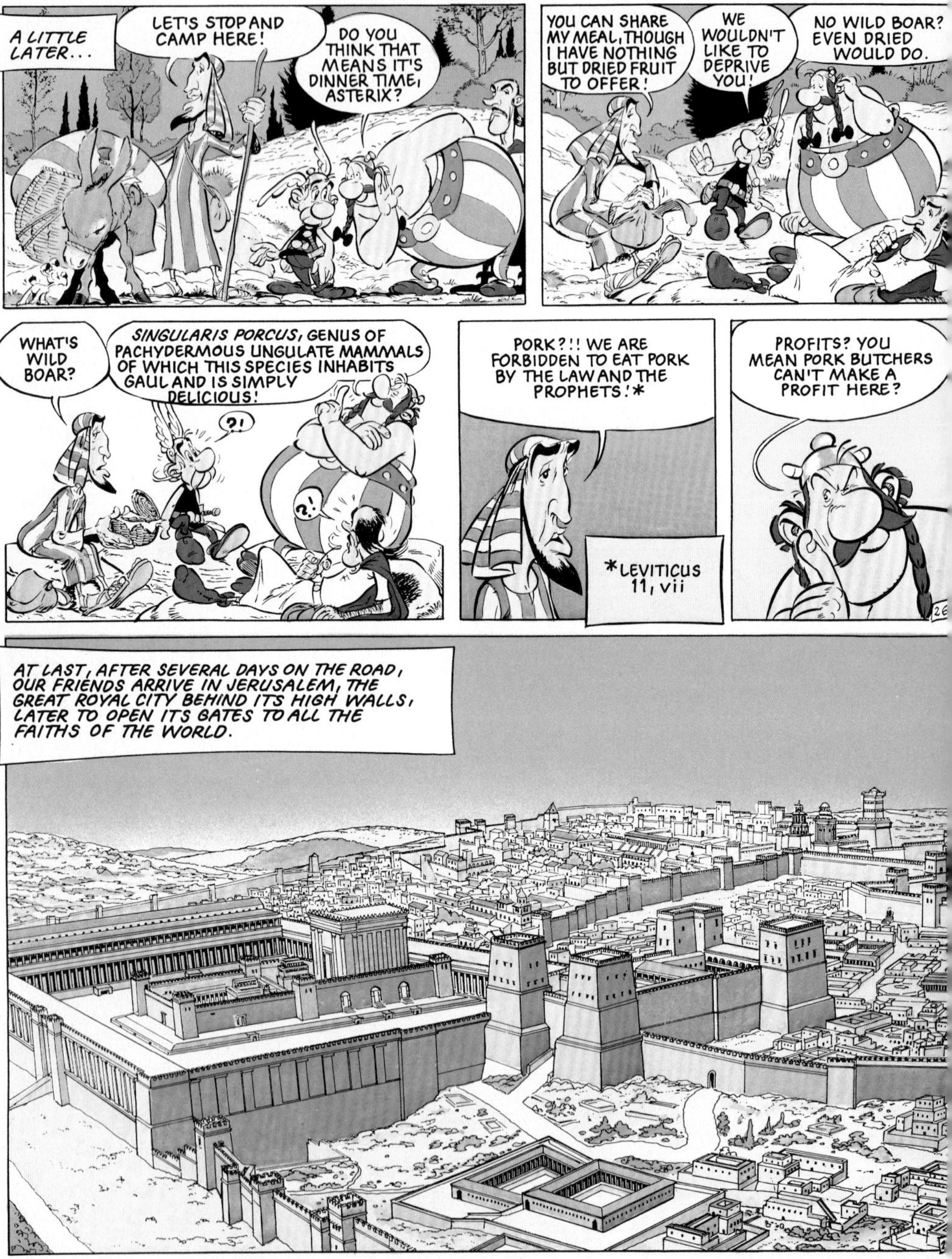

A LITTLE LATER...
LET'S STOP AND CAMP HERE!
DO YOU THINK THAT MEANS IT'S DINNER TIME, ASTERIX?
YOU CAN SHARE MY MEAL, THOUGH I HAVE NOTHING BUT DRIED FRUIT TO OFFER!
WE WOULDN'T LIKE TO DEPRIVE YOU!
NO WILD BOAR? EVEN DRIED WOULD DO.
WHAT'S WILD BOAR?
SINGULARIS PORCUS, GENUS OF PACHYDERMOUS UNGULATE MAMMALS OF WHICH THIS SPECIES INHABITS GAUL AND IS SIMPLY DELICIOUS!
?!
?!
PORK?!! WE ARE FORBIDDEN TO EAT PORK BY THE LAW AND THE PROPHETS!*
*LEVITICUS 11, vii
PROFITS? YOU MEAN PORK BUTCHERS CAN'T MAKE A PROFIT HERE?
AT LAST, AFTER SEVERAL DAYS ON THE ROAD, OUR FRIENDS ARRIVE IN JERUSALEM, THE GREAT ROYAL CITY BEHIND ITS HIGH WALLS, LATER TO OPEN ITS GATES TO ALL THE FAITHS OF THE WORLD.

SHALOM, ISAIAH! WHAT'S NEW?

NOTHING MUCH, EXCEPT THAT THE ROMANS HAVE DOUBLED THEIR GUARD AND ARE KEEPING A CLOSE WATCH ON ALL THE CITY GATES.

WHAT ARE THEY LOOKING FOR?

THREE GAULS AND A DOG, AND IF I WERE YOUR FRIENDS I'D WATCH MY STEP!

GOOD, SO THE FLY GOT THROUGH AGAIN!

WE'LL SAY GOODBYE. WE DON'T WANT TO BRING YOU TROUBLE!

BUT WHY ARE THE ROMANS AFTER YOU?

THEY'RE TRYING TO STOP US BUYING SOME ROCK OIL TO TAKE BACK TO GAUL!

SO NOW THEY'RE PLANNING TO PUT SMALL TRADERS OUT OF BUSINESS!

FOLLOW ME! I'LL TAKE YOU TO A FRIEND OF MINE IN A VILLAGE NEAR JERUSALEM. THE ROMANS WILL NEVER THINK OF LOOKING FOR YOU THERE!

AND TONIGHT WE'LL FIND SOME WAY TO GET YOU IN OVER THE WALLS!

WHY ARE YOU TAKING THE RISK OF HELPING US, JOSHUA?

ALL THE HEBREWS DISTRUST THE POWER OF ROME. WE MUST HELP THOSE WHO OPPOSE IT!

HERE WE ARE!

I NEVER SAW SUCH AN APPETITE! THAT'S HIS TENTH STUFFED CARP, AND HE STILL WANTS MORE!

IF YOU'D LIKE A REST, I CAN ONLY OFFER YOU THE STABLE, BUT YOU'LL FIND IT'S QUITE COMFORTABLE!

I'LL COME AND FETCH YOU TONIGHT!

LATER, AT NIGHT...

HE WAS RIGHT, IT IS COMFORTABLE. WHAT'S THIS VILLAGE CALLED?

BETHLEHEM, I THINK.

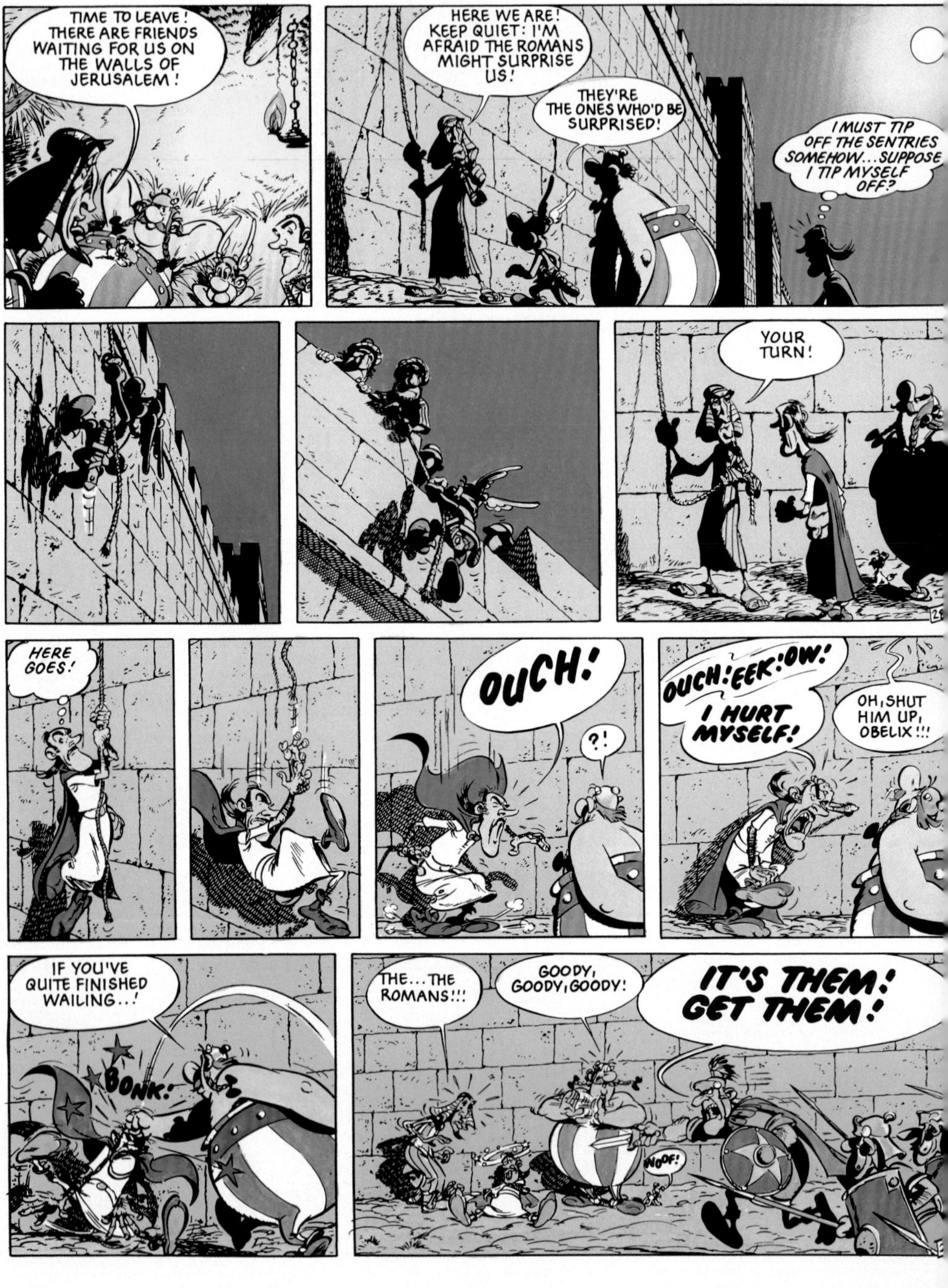
TIME TO LEAVE! THERE ARE FRIENDS WAITING FOR US ON THE WALLS OF JERUSALEM!
HERE WE ARE! KEEP QUIET: I'M AFRAID THE ROMANS MIGHT SURPRISE US!
THEY'RE THE ONES WHO'D BE SURPRISED!
I MUST TIP OFF THE SENTRIES SOMEHOW... SUPPOSE I TIP MYSELF OFF?
YOUR TURN!
HERE GOES!
OUCH!
?!
OUCH! EEK! OW! I HURT MYSELF!
OH, SHUT HIM UP, OBELIX!!!
IF YOU'VE QUITE FINISHED WAILING...!
BONK!
THE... THE ROMANS!!!
GOODY, GOODY, GOODY!
IT'S THEM! GET THEM!
WOOF!

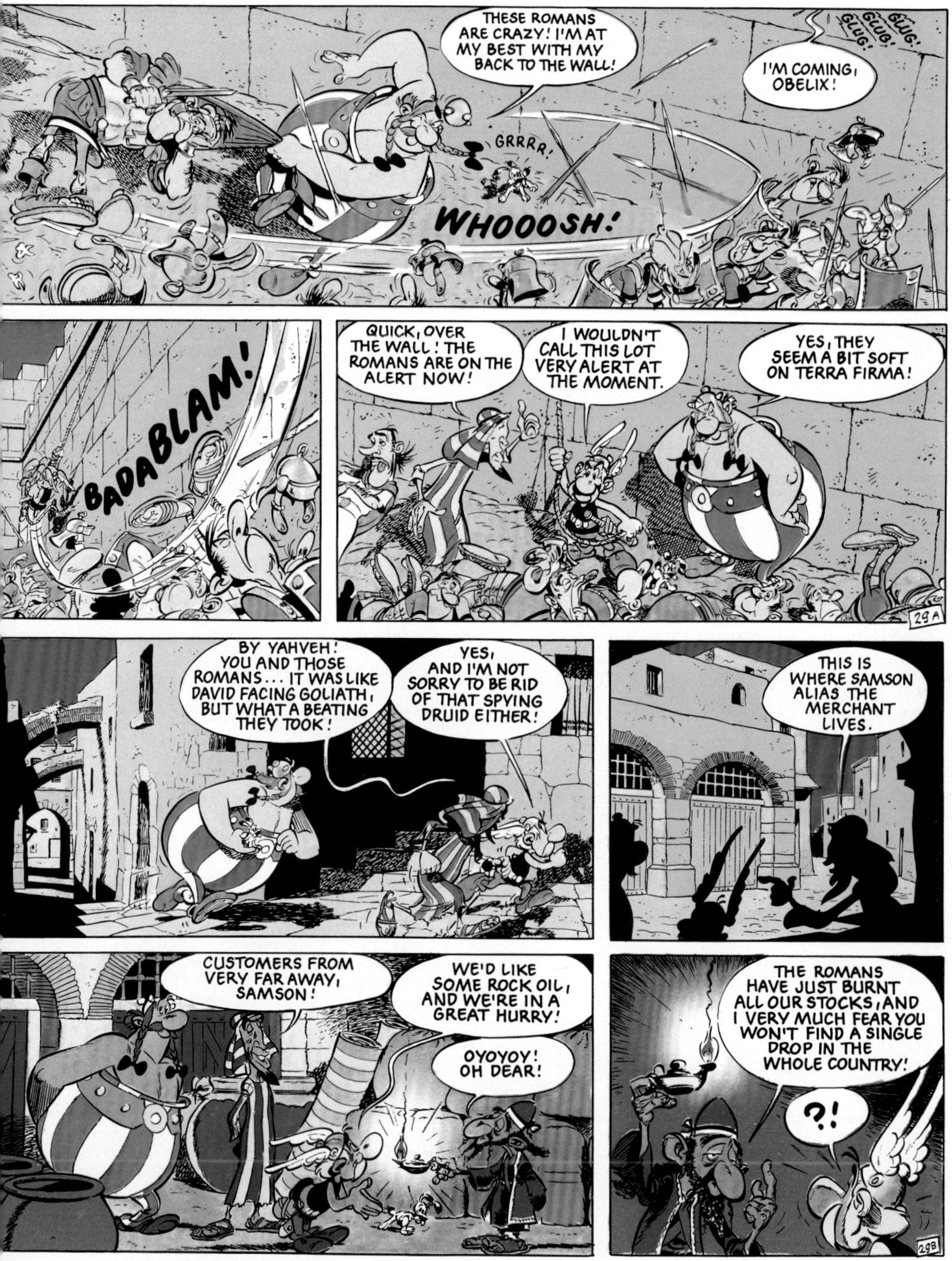

THESE ROMANS ARE CRAZY! I'M AT MY BEST WITH MY BACK TO THE WALL!
GLUG! GLUG! GLUG!
I'M COMING, OBELIX!
GRRRR!
WHOOOSH!
BADABLAM!
QUICK, OVER THE WALL! THE ROMANS ARE ON THE ALERT NOW!
I WOULDN'T CALL THIS LOT VERY ALERT AT THE MOMENT.
YES, THEY SEEM A BIT SOFT ON TERRA FIRMA!
29A
BY YAHVEH! YOU AND THOSE ROMANS... IT WAS LIKE DAVID FACING GOLIATH, BUT WHAT A BEATING THEY TOOK!
YES, AND I'M NOT SORRY TO BE RID OF THAT SPYING DRUID EITHER!
THIS IS WHERE SAMSON ALIAS THE MERCHANT LIVES.
CUSTOMERS FROM VERY FAR AWAY, SAMSON!
WE'D LIKE SOME ROCK OIL, AND WE'RE IN A GREAT HURRY!
OYOYOY! OH DEAR!
THE ROMANS HAVE JUST BURNT ALL OUR STOCKS, AND I VERY MUCH FEAR YOU WON'T FIND A SINGLE DROP IN THE WHOLE COUNTRY!
?!
29B

BUT WE MUST TAKE SOME ROCK OIL BACK TO GAUL! IT'S VITAL!

THEN YOU'LL HAVE TO LOOK WHERE THEY FIND IT: NEAR BABYLON IN MESOPOTAMIA!

HOW MANY MILES TO BABYLON?

WELL, IT'S THIRTY DAYS' JOURNEY, AND YOU'LL HAVE TO CROSS THE DESERT!

I'VE NEVER TRIED A DESERT CROSSING BEFORE BUT BY TOUTATIS, I'M READY TO TACKLE IT!

HERE'S MY ASSISTANT, SAUL BEN EPHISHUL. AT SUNRISE HE WILL GUIDE YOU TO THE EDGE OF THE DESERT.

WEAR THESE AND YOU'LL PASS UNNOTICED.

HOW CAN WE THANK YOU?

OH, IF YOU'RE AIMING TO GIVE THE ROMANS TROUBLE, WE'RE QUITS!

BUT YOUR OWN NAME SOUNDS RATHER ROMAN, SAMSON ALIUS?

I TOOK THIS ALIAS FOR BUSINESS REASONS. MY REAL NAME IS ROSEN-BLUMENTHALOVITCH

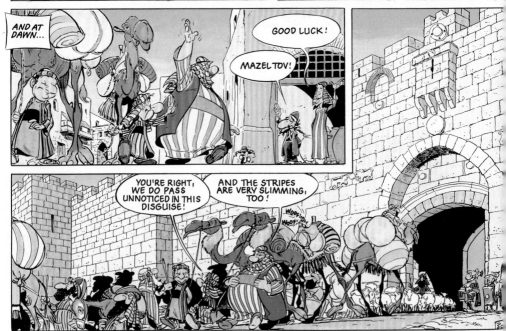

AND AT DAWN...

GOOD LUCK!

MAZEL TOV!

YOU'RE RIGHT, WE DO PASS UNNOTICED IN THIS DISGUISE!

AND THE STRIPES ARE VERY SLIMMING, TOO!

WOOF! WOOF!

34

AT THE ROMAN PROCURATOR'S PALACE...

AVE, O PONTIUS PIRATE! THE GAULS GOT AWAY, AND WE FEAR THEY'VE MADE GOOD THEIR ESCAPE NOW!

ONCE THEY'RE OUTSIDE MY TERRITORY, MY DEAR DUBBEL-OSIX, I COULDN'T CARE LESS WHAT THEY DO!

I WISH HE'D STOP WASHING HIS HANDS THE WHOLE TIME!

WELL, NEVER MIND! ASTERIX AND OBELIX ARE BOUND TO GO BACK ON BOARD SHIP, AND WHEN THEY DO WE'LL BE WAITING, WITH QUITE A RECEPTION COMMITTEE!

MEANWHILE...

WE'RE COMING TO THE DEAD SEA!

IT MAKES ME SICK, ASTERIX!

I HAVE TO ADMIT THESE MOUNTS ARE RATHER BUMPY!

I DIDN'T MEAN THAT! IT MAKES ME SICK TO THINK OF THE RACIAL DISCRIMI— NATION PRACTISED AGAINST BOARS IN THIS COUNTRY!

?!?

31A

THE SEA! YIPPEE!!!

IT'S SO HOT, I COULD DO WITH A NICE DIP!

HEY, WAIT!

HERE GOES!

?

FLOP! FLOP! FLOP! FLOP!

I WAS GOING TO WARN YOU: THE DEAD SEA HAS A SALT CONTENT SIX TIMES HIGHER THAN THAT OF OTHER SEAS, AND ITS DENSITY IS SUCH THAT THE HUMAN BODY JUST FLOATS ON TOP!

HOHOHO! HAHA!

ARF! ARF! ARF!

31B

35

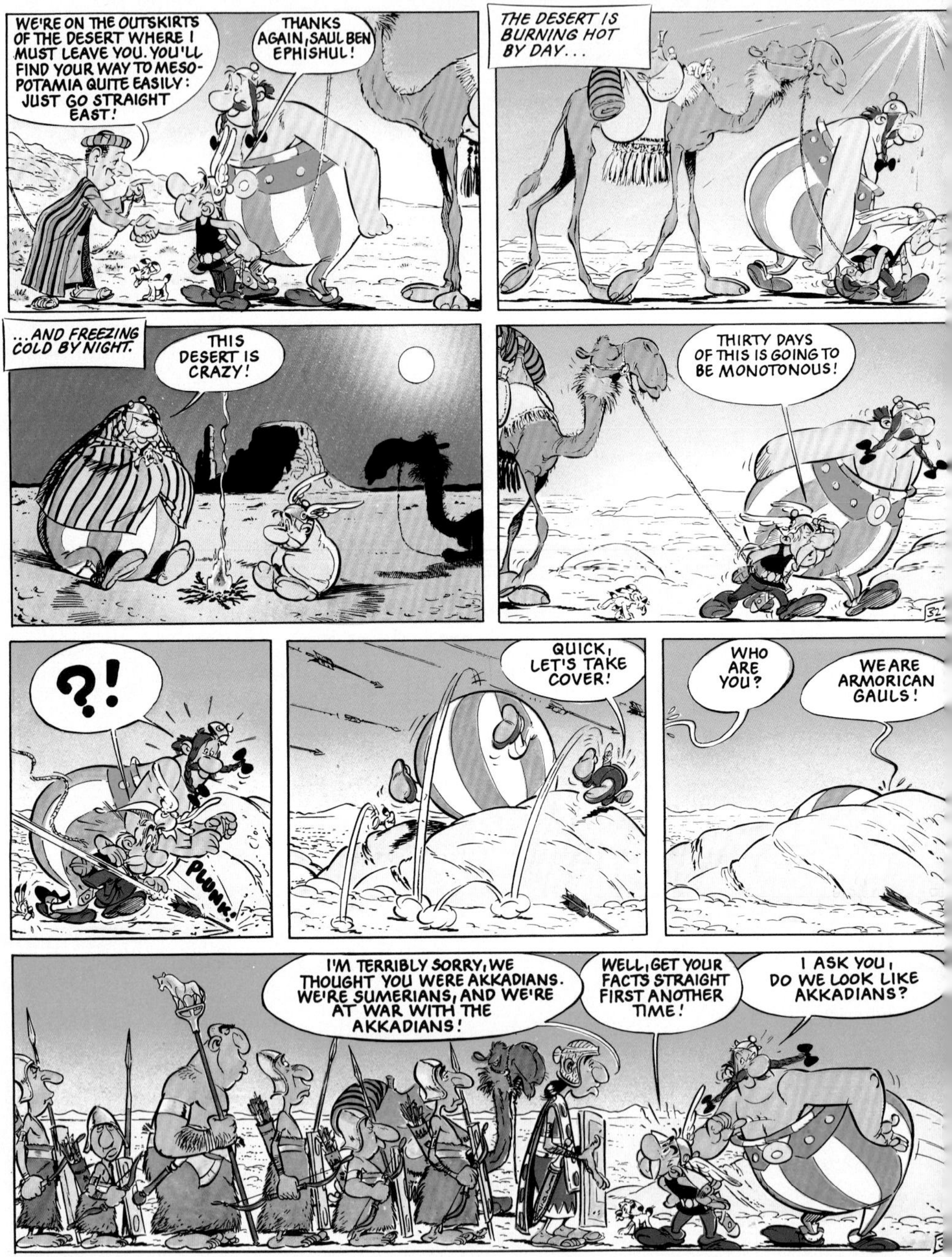
WE'RE ON THE OUTSKIRTS OF THE DESERT WHERE I MUST LEAVE YOU. YOU'LL FIND YOUR WAY TO MESO-POTAMIA QUITE EASILY: JUST GO STRAIGHT EAST!
THANKS AGAIN, SAUL BEN EPHISHUL!
THE DESERT IS BURNING HOT BY DAY...
...AND FREEZING COLD BY NIGHT.
THIS DESERT IS CRAZY!
THIRTY DAYS OF THIS IS GOING TO BE MONOTONOUS!
?!
PLUNK!
QUICK, LET'S TAKE COVER!
WHO ARE YOU?
WE ARE ARMORICAN GAULS!
I'M TERRIBLY SORRY, WE THOUGHT YOU WERE AKKADIANS. WE'RE SUMERIANS, AND WE'RE AT WAR WITH THE AKKADIANS!
WELL, GET YOUR FACTS STRAIGHT FIRST ANOTHER TIME!
I ASK YOU, DO WE LOOK LIKE AKKADIANS?

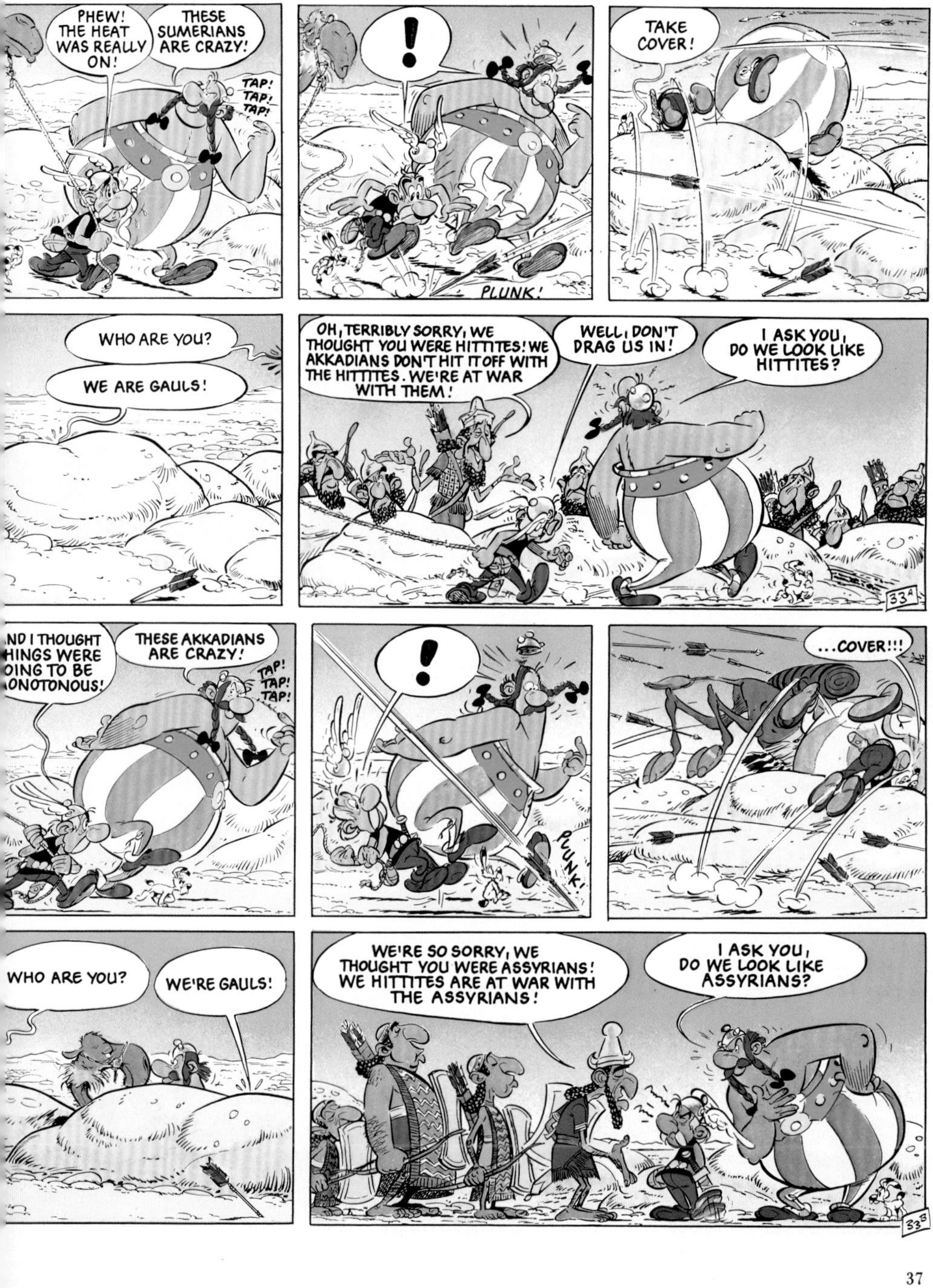
PHEW! THE HEAT WAS REALLY ON!
THESE SUMERIANS ARE CRAZY!
TAP! TAP! TAP!
!
PLUNK!
TAKE COVER!
WHO ARE YOU?
WE ARE GAULS!
OH, TERRIBLY SORRY, WE THOUGHT YOU WERE HITTITES! WE AKKADIANS DON'T HIT IT OFF WITH THE HITTITES. WE'RE AT WAR WITH THEM!
WELL, DON'T DRAG US IN!
I ASK YOU, DO WE LOOK LIKE HITTITES?
33A
ND I THOUGHT HINGS WERE OING TO BE ONOTONOUS!
THESE AKKADIANS ARE CRAZY!
TAP! TAP! TAP!
!
PLUNK!
...COVER!!!
WHO ARE YOU?
WE'RE GAULS!
WE'RE SO SORRY, WE THOUGHT YOU WERE ASSYRIANS! WE HITTITES ARE AT WAR WITH THE ASSYRIANS!
I ASK YOU, DO WE LOOK LIKE ASSYRIANS?
33B

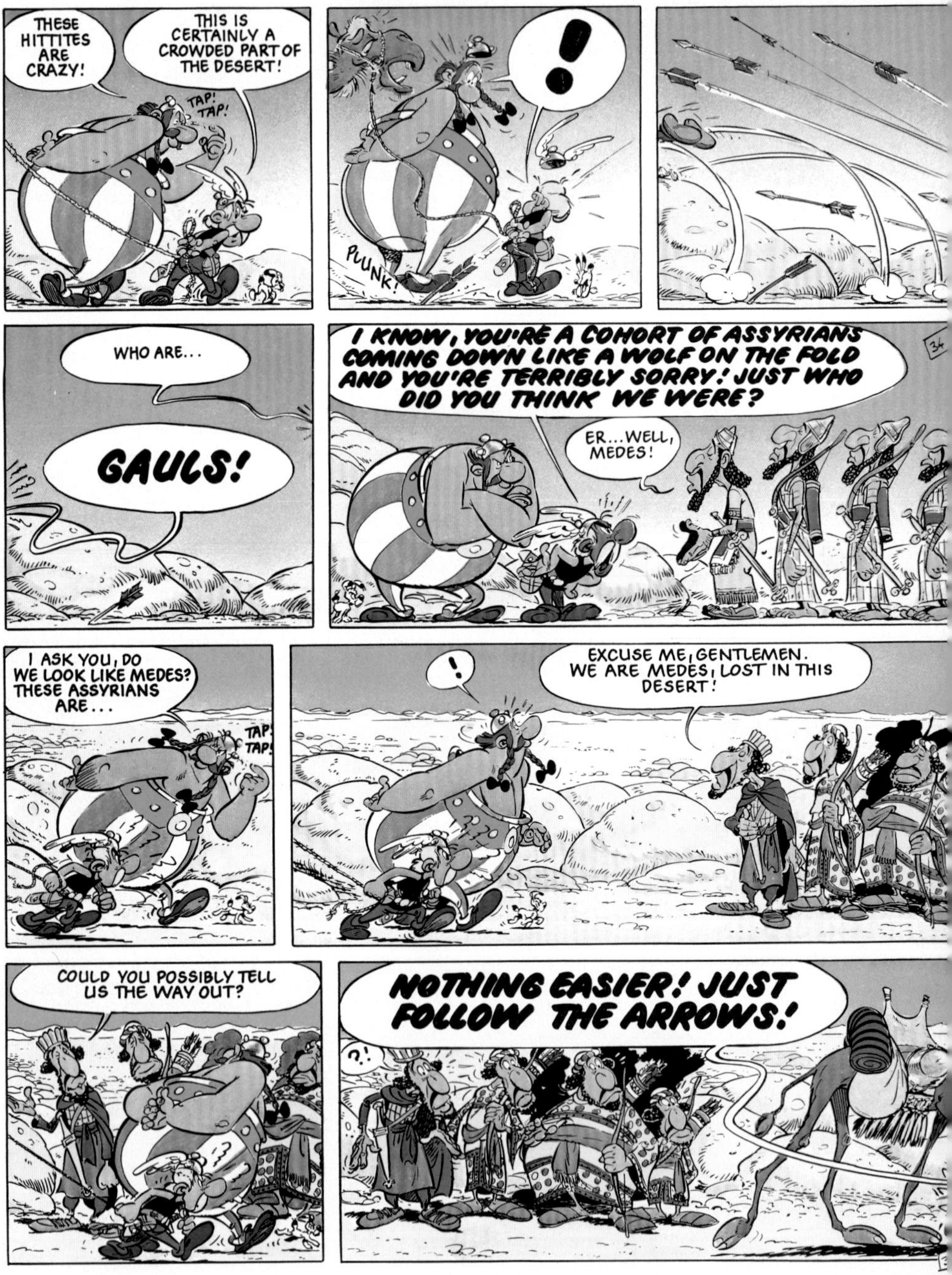
THESE HITTITES ARE CRAZY!
THIS IS CERTAINLY A CROWDED PART OF THE DESERT!
TAP! TAP!
!
PLUNK!
WHO ARE...
GAULS!
I KNOW, YOU'RE A COHORT OF ASSYRIANS COMING DOWN LIKE A WOLF ON THE FOLD AND YOU'RE TERRIBLY SORRY! JUST WHO DID YOU THINK WE WERE?
ER...WELL, MEDES!
I ASK YOU, DO WE LOOK LIKE MEDES? THESE ASSYRIANS ARE...
TAP! TAP!
!
EXCUSE ME, GENTLEMEN. WE ARE MEDES, LOST IN THIS DESERT!
COULD YOU POSSIBLY TELL US THE WAY OUT?
NOTHING EASIER! JUST FOLLOW THE ARROWS!
?!

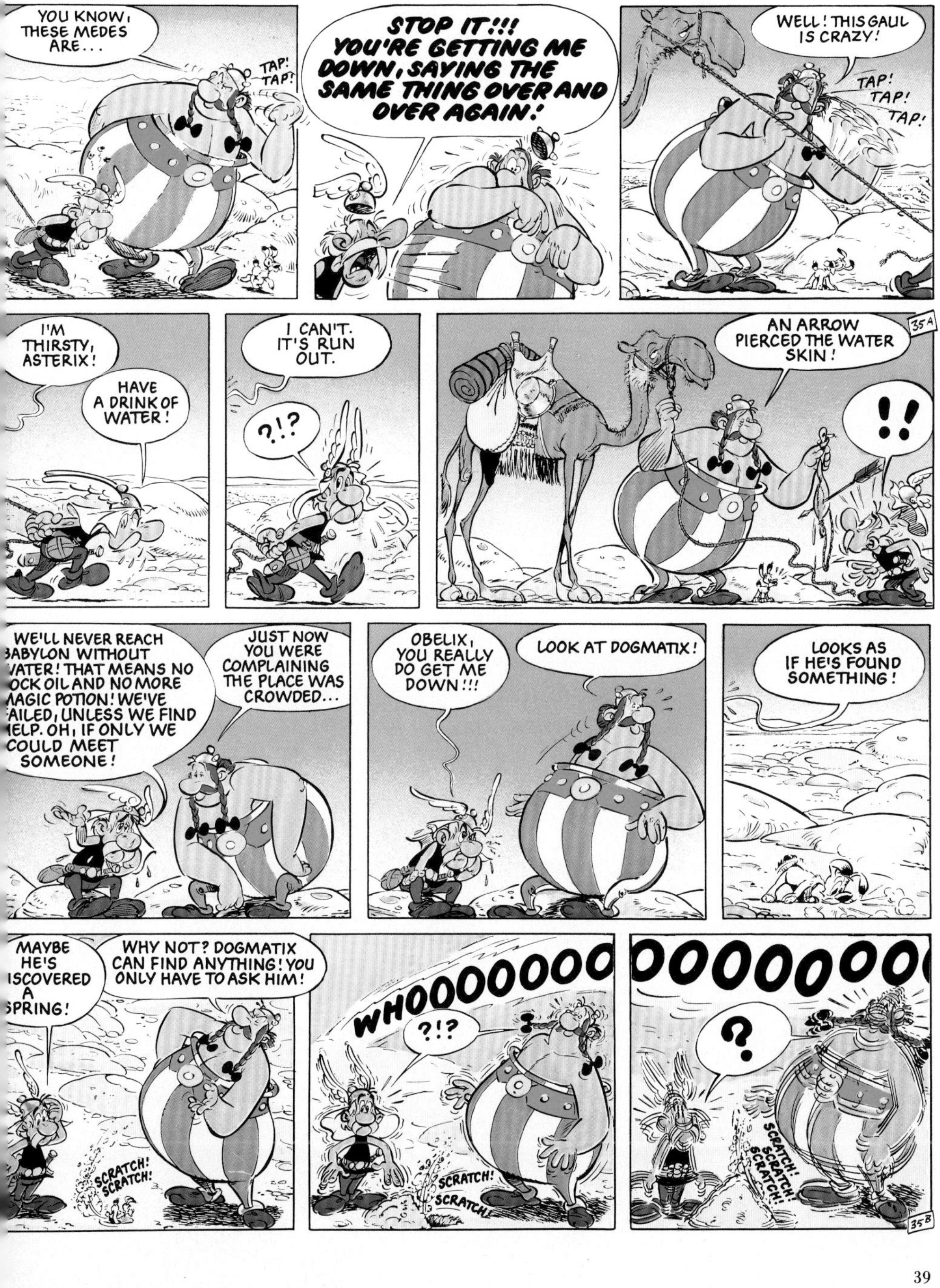

YOU KNOW, THESE MEDES ARE...
TAP! TAP!
STOP IT!!! YOU'RE GETTING ME DOWN, SAYING THE SAME THING OVER AND OVER AGAIN!
WELL! THIS GAUL IS CRAZY!
TAP! TAP! TAP!
I'M THIRSTY, ASTERIX!
HAVE A DRINK OF WATER!
I CAN'T. IT'S RUN OUT.
?!?
AN ARROW PIERCED THE WATER SKIN!
!!
WE'LL NEVER REACH BABYLON WITHOUT WATER! THAT MEANS NO ROCK OIL AND NO MORE MAGIC POTION! WE'VE FAILED, UNLESS WE FIND HELP. OH, IF ONLY WE COULD MEET SOMEONE!
JUST NOW YOU WERE COMPLAINING THE PLACE WAS CROWDED...
OBELIX, YOU REALLY DO GET ME DOWN!!!
LOOK AT DOGMATIX!
LOOKS AS IF HE'S FOUND SOMETHING!
MAYBE HE'S DISCOVERED A SPRING!
WHY NOT? DOGMATIX CAN FIND ANYTHING! YOU ONLY HAVE TO ASK HIM!
SCRATCH! SCRATCH!
WHOOOOOOOO
?!?
SCRATCH! SCRATCH!
OOOOOOOO
?
SCRATCH! SCRATCH! SCRATCH!

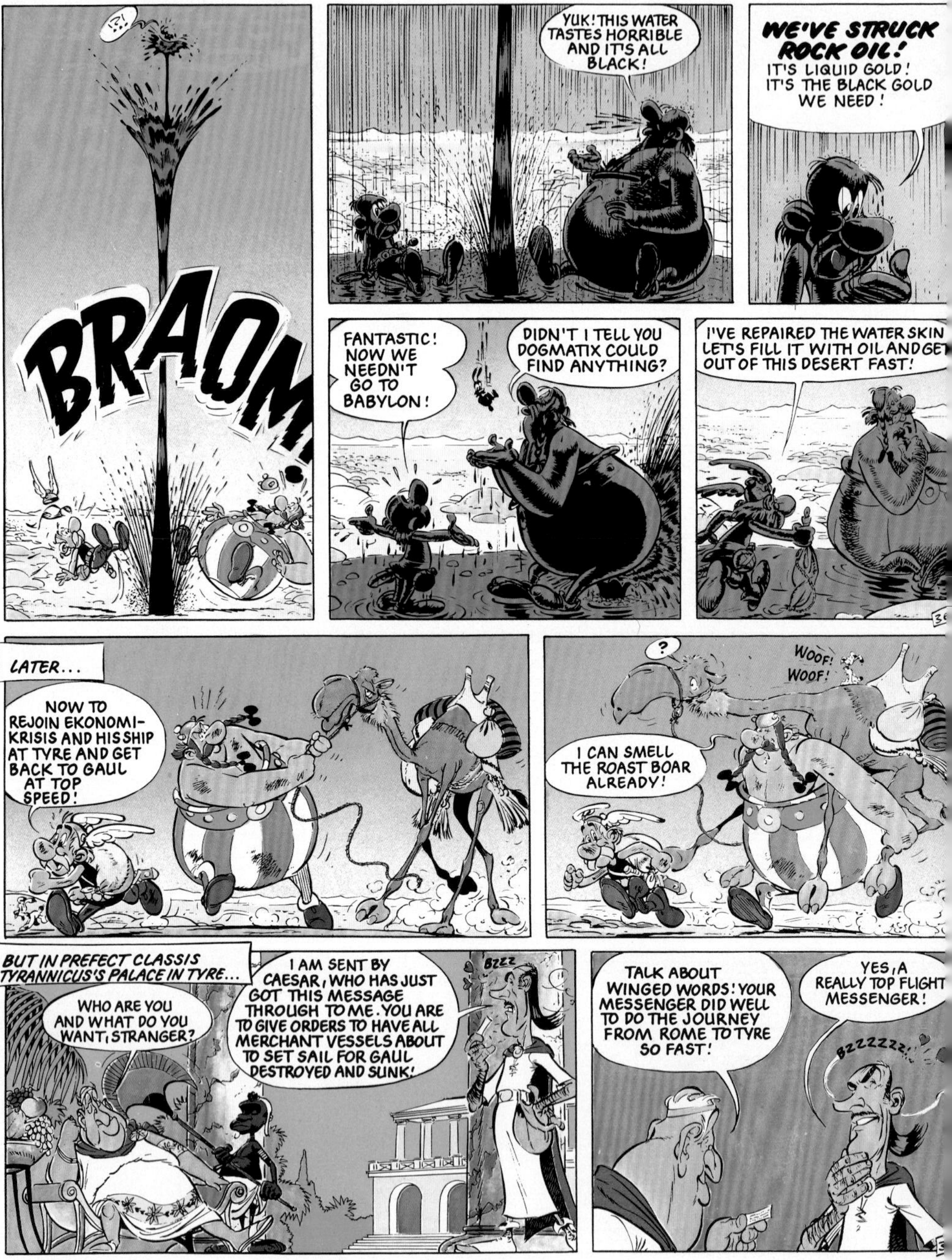
?!
BRAOM
YUK! THIS WATER TASTES HORRIBLE AND IT'S ALL BLACK!
WE'VE STRUCK ROCK OIL!
IT'S LIQUID GOLD! IT'S THE BLACK GOLD WE NEED!
FANTASTIC! NOW WE NEEDN'T GO TO BABYLON!
DIDN'T I TELL YOU DOGMATIX COULD FIND ANYTHING?
I'VE REPAIRED THE WATER SKIN LET'S FILL IT WITH OIL AND GET OUT OF THIS DESERT FAST!
LATER...
NOW TO REJOIN EKONOMIKRISIS AND HIS SHIP AT TYRE AND GET BACK TO GAUL AT TOP SPEED!
?
WOOF! WOOF!
I CAN SMELL THE ROAST BOAR ALREADY!
BUT IN PREFECT CLASSIS TYRANNICUS'S PALACE IN TYRE...
WHO ARE YOU AND WHAT DO YOU WANT, STRANGER?
I AM SENT BY CAESAR, WHO HAS JUST GOT THIS MESSAGE THROUGH TO ME. YOU ARE TO GIVE ORDERS TO HAVE ALL MERCHANT VESSELS ABOUT TO SET SAIL FOR GAUL DESTROYED AND SUNK!
BZZZ
TALK ABOUT WINGED WORDS: YOUR MESSENGER DID WELL TO DO THE JOURNEY FROM ROME TO TYRE SO FAST!
YES, A REALLY TOP FLIGHT MESSENGER!
BZZZZZZ

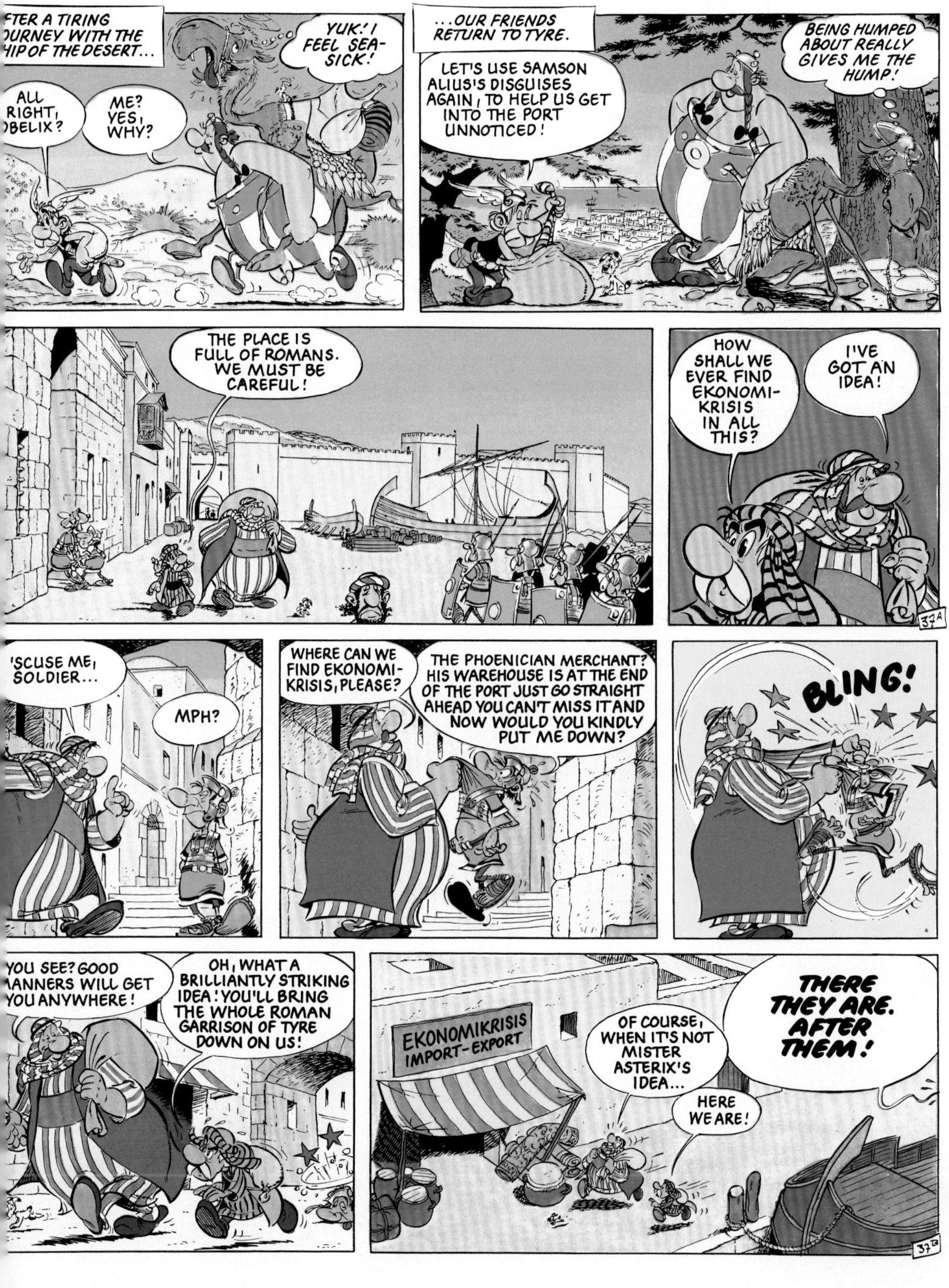

FTER A TIRING
OURNEY WITH THE
HIP OF THE DESERT...
YUK! I FEEL SEA-SICK!
ALL RIGHT, OBELIX?
ME? YES, WHY?
...OUR FRIENDS RETURN TO TYRE.
LET'S USE SAMSON ALIUS'S DISGUISES AGAIN, TO HELP US GET INTO THE PORT UNNOTICED!
BEING HUMPED ABOUT REALLY GIVES ME THE HUMP!
THE PLACE IS FULL OF ROMANS. WE MUST BE CAREFUL!
HOW SHALL WE EVER FIND EKONOMI-KRISIS IN ALL THIS?
I'VE GOT AN IDEA!
37A
'SCUSE ME, SOLDIER...
MPH?
WHERE CAN WE FIND EKONOMI-KRISIS, PLEASE?
THE PHOENICIAN MERCHANT? HIS WAREHOUSE IS AT THE END OF THE PORT JUST GO STRAIGHT AHEAD YOU CAN'T MISS IT AND NOW WOULD YOU KINDLY PUT ME DOWN?
BLING!
YOU SEE? GOOD
ANNERS WILL GET
YOU ANYWHERE!
OH, WHAT A BRILLIANTLY STRIKING IDEA! YOU'LL BRING THE WHOLE ROMAN GARRISON OF TYRE DOWN ON US!
EKONOMIKRISIS IMPORT-EXPORT
OF COURSE, WHEN IT'S NOT MISTER ASTERIX'S IDEA...
HERE WE ARE!
THERE THEY ARE. AFTER THEM!
37B

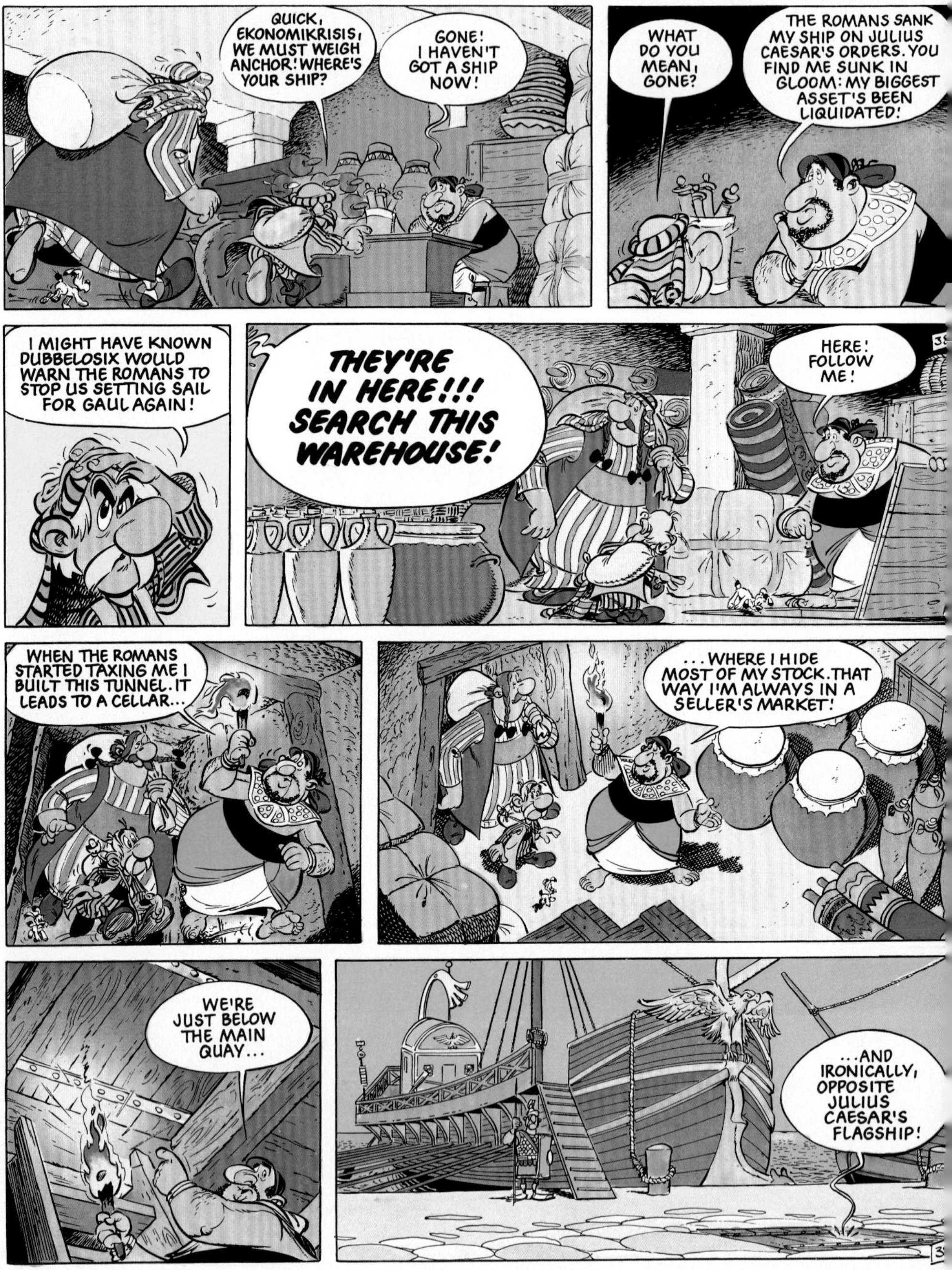
QUICK, EKONOMIKRISIS, WE MUST WEIGH ANCHOR! WHERE'S YOUR SHIP?
GONE! I HAVEN'T GOT A SHIP NOW!
WHAT DO YOU MEAN, GONE?
THE ROMANS SANK MY SHIP ON JULIUS CAESAR'S ORDERS. YOU FIND ME SUNK IN GLOOM: MY BIGGEST ASSET'S BEEN LIQUIDATED!
I MIGHT HAVE KNOWN DUBBELOSIX WOULD WARN THE ROMANS TO STOP US SETTING SAIL FOR GAUL AGAIN!
THEY'RE IN HERE!!! SEARCH THIS WAREHOUSE!
HERE! FOLLOW ME!
WHEN THE ROMANS STARTED TAXING ME I BUILT THIS TUNNEL. IT LEADS TO A CELLAR...
...WHERE I HIDE MOST OF MY STOCK. THAT WAY I'M ALWAYS IN A SELLER'S MARKET!
WE'RE JUST BELOW THE MAIN QUAY...
...AND IRONICALLY, OPPOSITE JULIUS CAESAR'S FLAGSHIP!

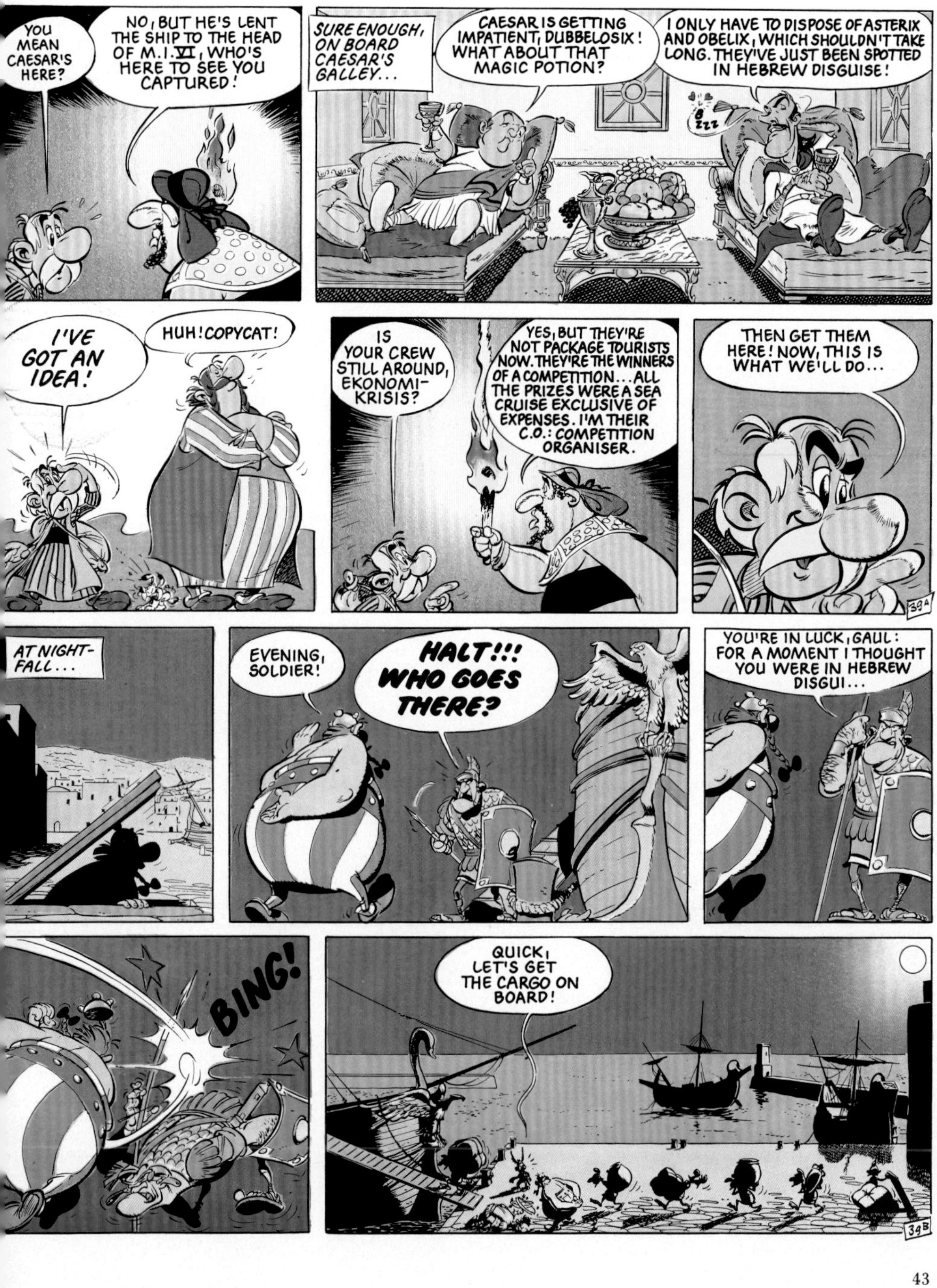
YOU MEAN CAESAR'S HERE?
NO, BUT HE'S LENT THE SHIP TO THE HEAD OF M.I.VI, WHO'S HERE TO SEE YOU CAPTURED!
SURE ENOUGH, ON BOARD CAESAR'S GALLEY...
CAESAR IS GETTING IMPATIENT, DUBBELOSIX! WHAT ABOUT THAT MAGIC POTION?
I ONLY HAVE TO DISPOSE OF ASTERIX AND OBELIX, WHICH SHOULDN'T TAKE LONG. THEY'VE JUST BEEN SPOTTED IN HEBREW DISGUISE!
I'VE GOT AN IDEA!
HUH! COPYCAT!
IS YOUR CREW STILL AROUND, EKONOMIKRISIS?
YES, BUT THEY'RE NOT PACKAGE TOURISTS NOW. THEY'RE THE WINNERS OF A COMPETITION... ALL THE PRIZES WERE A SEA CRUISE EXCLUSIVE OF EXPENSES. I'M THEIR C.O.: COMPETITION ORGANISER.
THEN GET THEM HERE! NOW, THIS IS WHAT WE'LL DO...
39A
AT NIGHTFALL...
EVENING, SOLDIER!
HALT!!! WHO GOES THERE?
YOU'RE IN LUCK, GAUL: FOR A MOMENT I THOUGHT YOU WERE IN HEBREW DISGUI...
BING!
QUICK, LET'S GET THE CARGO ON BOARD!
39B

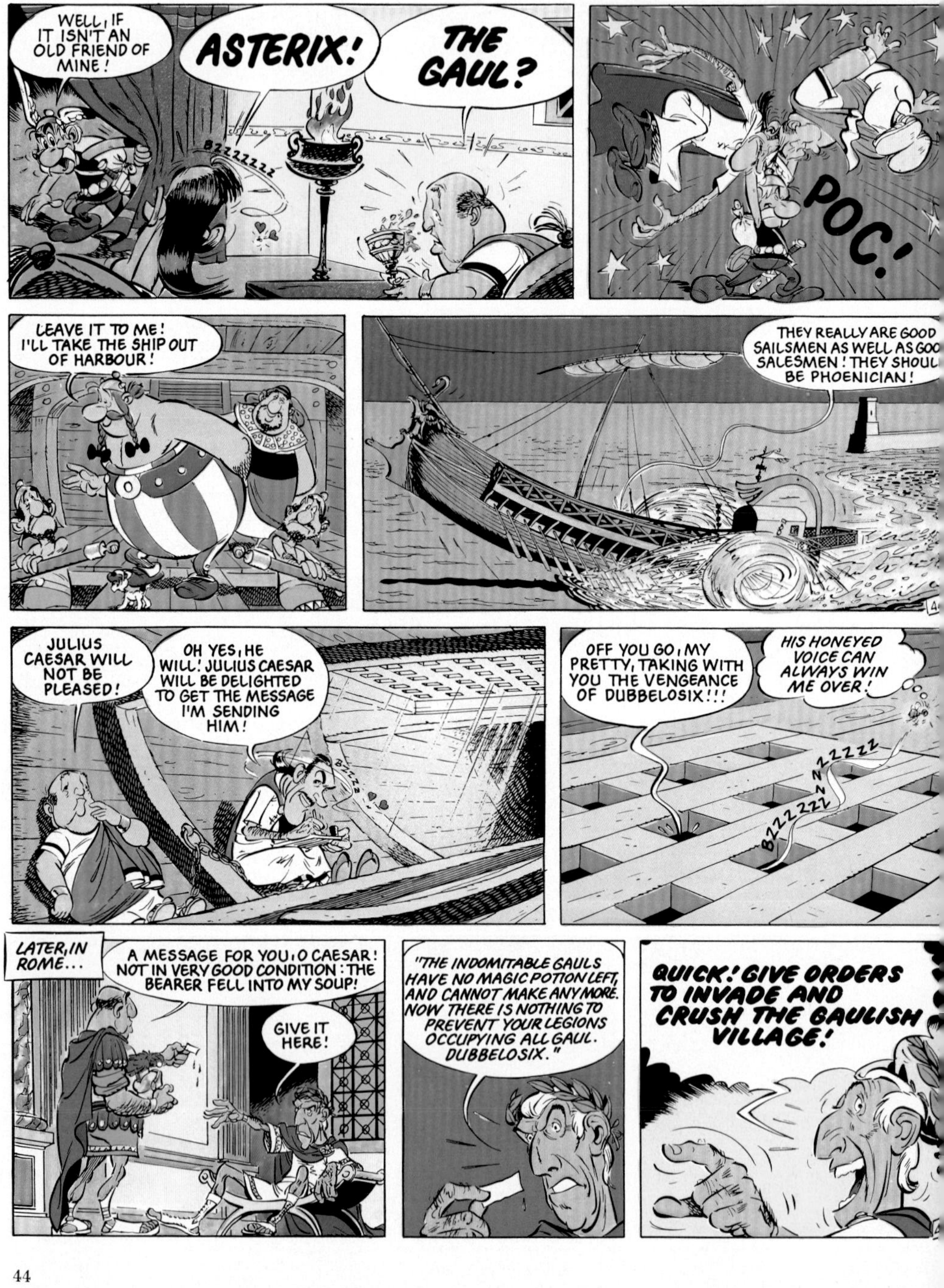
WELL, IF IT ISN'T AN OLD FRIEND OF MINE!
ASTERIX!
THE GAUL?
BZZZZZZZZ
POC!
LEAVE IT TO ME! I'LL TAKE THE SHIP OUT OF HARBOUR!
THEY REALLY ARE GOOD SAILSMEN AS WELL AS GOO SALESMEN! THEY SHOUL BE PHOENICIAN!
JULIUS CAESAR WILL NOT BE PLEASED!
OH YES, HE WILL! JULIUS CAESAR WILL BE DELIGHTED TO GET THE MESSAGE I'M SENDING HIM!
OFF YOU GO, MY PRETTY, TAKING WITH YOU THE VENGEANCE OF DUBBELOSIX!!!
HIS HONEYED VOICE CAN ALWAYS WIN ME OVER!
BZZZZZZZZZZZZZ
LATER, IN ROME...
A MESSAGE FOR YOU, O CAESAR! NOT IN VERY GOOD CONDITION: THE BEARER FELL INTO MY SOUP!
GIVE IT HERE!
"THE INDOMITABLE GAULS HAVE NO MAGIC POTION LEFT, AND CANNOT MAKE ANYMORE. NOW THERE IS NOTHING TO PREVENT YOUR LEGIONS OCCUPYING ALL GAUL. DUBBELOSIX."
QUICK! GIVE ORDERS TO INVADE AND CRUSH THE GAULISH VILLAGE!

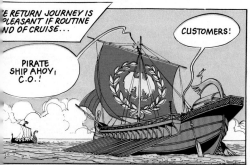

THE RETURN JOURNEY IS PLEASANT IF ROUTINE... END OF CRUISE...

PIRATE SHIP AHOY, C.O.!

CUSTOMERS!

ROMAN GALLEY TO STARBOARD!

WE'RE NEUTRAL! EVERYONE KNOWS THAT! I WAIVE THIS ONE... LET THE ROMANS RULE THE WAVES!

BUT THEY'RE NOT WAVERING! THEY'RE GIVING CHASE!

?!

...TER...

FOUR THOUSAND SESTERTII! THAT'S IT!

BUT THAT'S TWICE LAST TIME'S PRICE!

YOU KNOW HOW IT IS WITH THE INFLATION!

HOW WOULD YOU LIKE TO GO INTO BUSINESS WITH ME!

AVE ATQUE VALE!

NEVER MIND THE VEILED REFERENCES, HOW AM I GOING TO SELL THIS LOT?

FLOAT A COMPANY!

41A

WELL, WE ARE BRINGING ROCK OIL BACK TO GAUL IN SPITE OF YOU, DUBBELOSIX!

?!

I'M NOT SO SURE ABOUT THAT!

NO, OBELIX! NOOOO!

PRRRFFFFF

BONG!

WOOF! WOOF!

AND THE WATERS OF THE CHANNEL ARE POLLUTED FOR THE FIRST TIME IN HISTORY.

OH NO! DON'T SAY YOU'RE STARTING ALREADY?!

41B

45

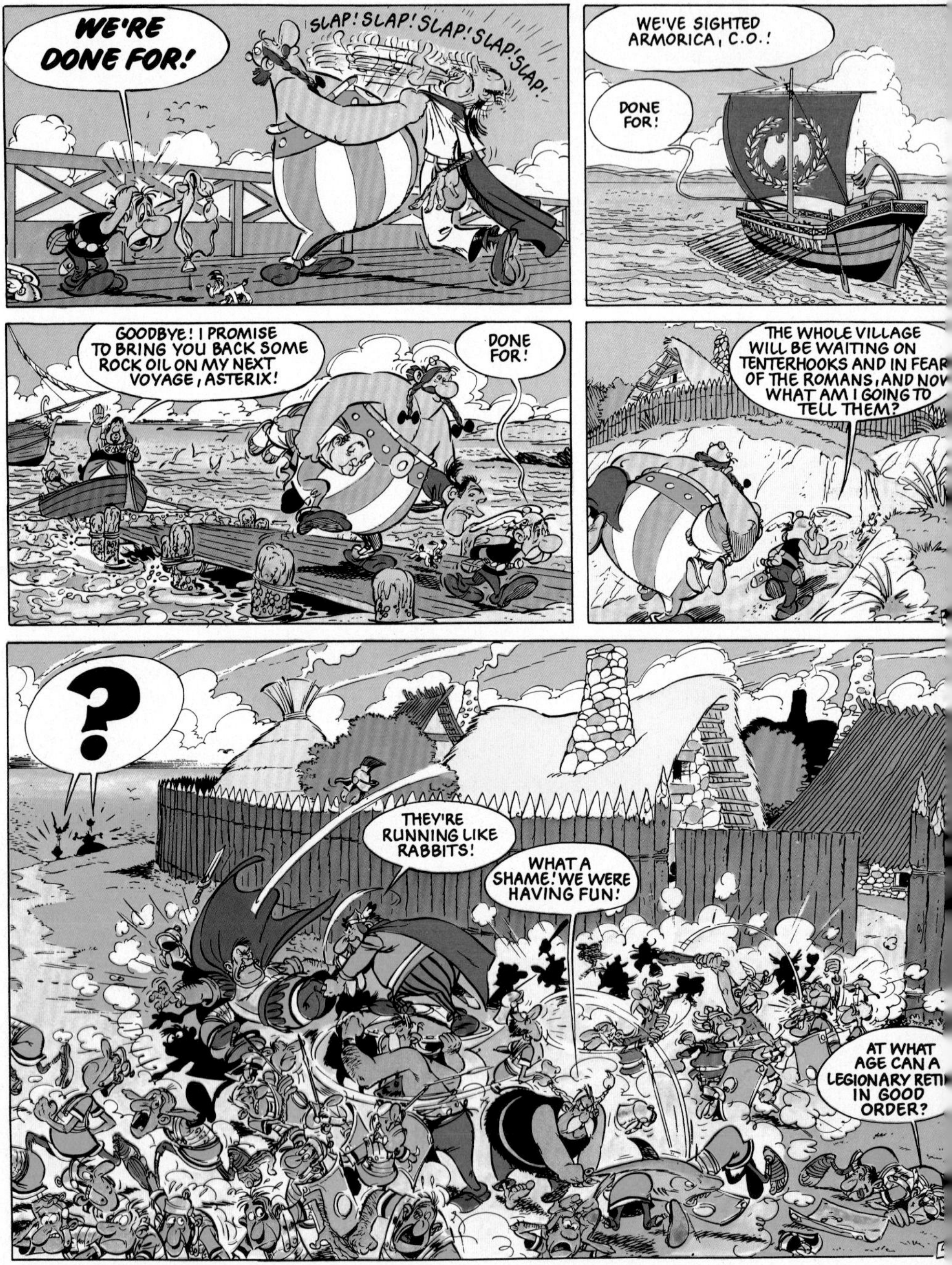
WE'RE DONE FOR!
SLAP! SLAP! SLAP! SLAP! SLAP! SLAP!
WE'VE SIGHTED ARMORICA, C.O.!
DONE FOR!
GOODBYE! I PROMISE TO BRING YOU BACK SOME ROCK OIL ON MY NEXT VOYAGE, ASTERIX!
DONE FOR!
THE WHOLE VILLAGE WILL BE WAITING ON TENTERHOOKS AND IN FEAR OF THE ROMANS, AND NO
WHAT AM I GOING TO TELL THEM?
?
THEY'RE RUNNING LIKE RABBITS!
WHAT A SHAME! WE WERE HAVING FUN!
AT WHAT AGE CAN A LEGIONARY RETI
IN GOOD ORDER?

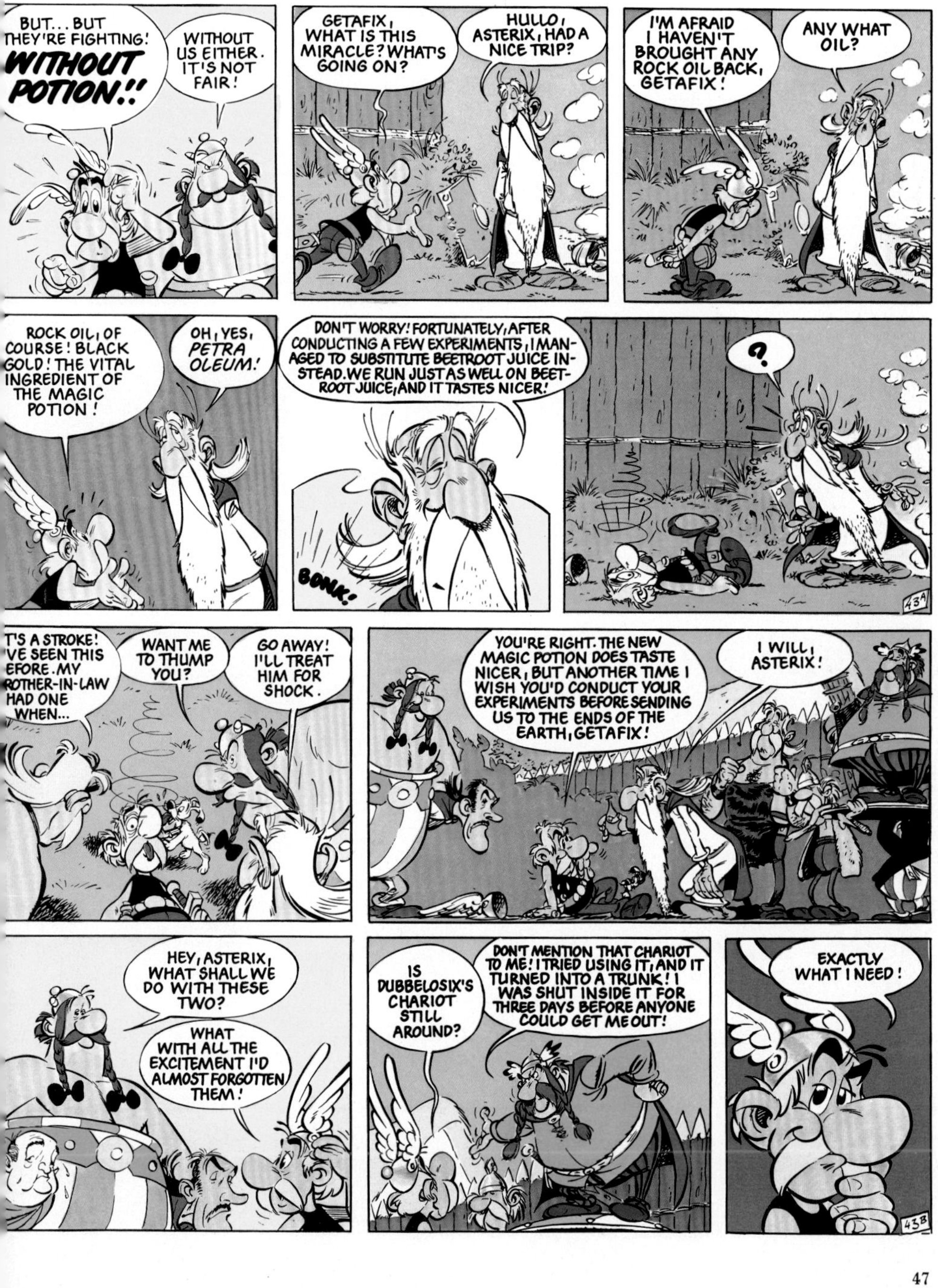
BUT... BUT THEY'RE FIGHTING! WITHOUT POTION.!!
WITHOUT US EITHER. IT'S NOT FAIR!
GETAFIX, WHAT IS THIS MIRACLE? WHAT'S GOING ON?
HULLO, ASTERIX, HAD A NICE TRIP?
I'M AFRAID I HAVEN'T BROUGHT ANY ROCK OIL BACK, GETAFIX!
ANY WHAT OIL?
ROCK OIL, OF COURSE! BLACK GOLD! THE VITAL INGREDIENT OF THE MAGIC POTION!
OH, YES, PETRA OLEUM!
DON'T WORRY! FORTUNATELY, AFTER CONDUCTING A FEW EXPERIMENTS, I MANAGED TO SUBSTITUTE BEETROOT JUICE INSTEAD. WE RUN JUST AS WELL ON BEETROOT JUICE, AND IT TASTES NICER!
BONK!
?
43A
T'S A STROKE! 'VE SEEN THIS EFORE. MY ROTHER-IN-LAW HAD ONE WHEN...
WANT ME TO THUMP YOU?
GO AWAY! I'LL TREAT HIM FOR SHOCK.
YOU'RE RIGHT. THE NEW MAGIC POTION DOES TASTE NICER, BUT ANOTHER TIME I WISH YOU'D CONDUCT YOUR EXPERIMENTS BEFORE SENDING US TO THE ENDS OF THE EARTH, GETAFIX!
I WILL, ASTERIX!
HEY, ASTERIX, WHAT SHALL WE DO WITH THESE TWO?
WHAT WITH ALL THE EXCITEMENT I'D ALMOST FORGOTTEN THEM!
IS DUBBELOSIX'S CHARIOT STILL AROUND?
DON'T MENTION THAT CHARIOT TO ME! I TRIED USING IT, AND IT TURNED INTO A TRUNK! I WAS SHUT INSIDE IT FOR THREE DAYS BEFORE ANYONE COULD GET ME OUT!
EXACTLY WHAT I NEED!
43B

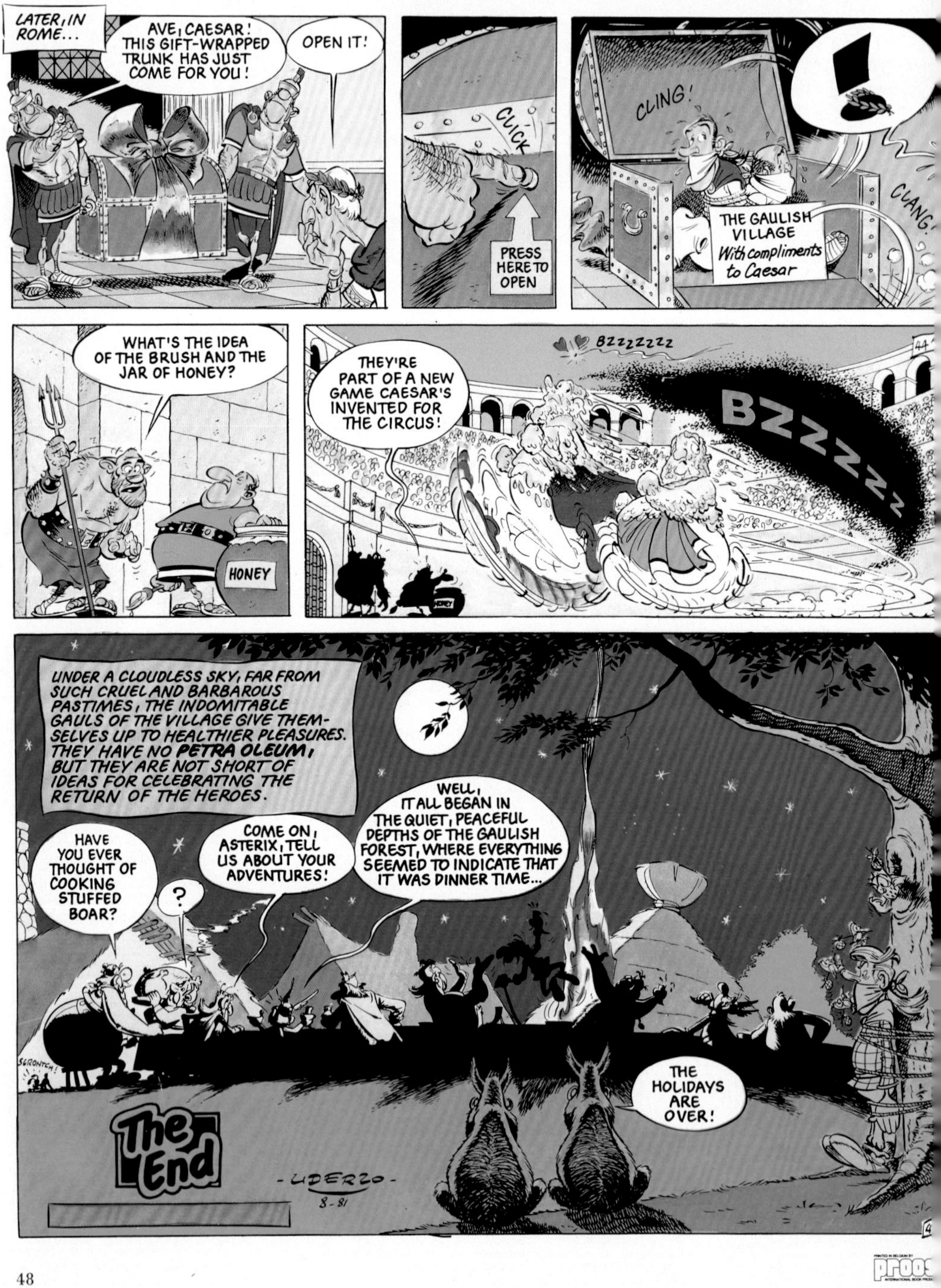
LATER, IN ROME...
AVE, CAESAR! THIS GIFT-WRAPPED TRUNK HAS JUST COME FOR YOU!
OPEN IT!
CLICK
PRESS HERE TO OPEN
CLING!
!
CLANG!
THE GAULISH VILLAGE With compliments to Caesar
WHAT'S THE IDEA OF THE BRUSH AND THE JAR OF HONEY?
HONEY
THEY'RE PART OF A NEW GAME CAESAR'S INVENTED FOR THE CIRCUS!
BZZZZZZZ
BZZZZZZ
44
UNDER A CLOUDLESS SKY, FAR FROM SUCH CRUEL AND BARBAROUS PASTIMES, THE INDOMITABLE GAULS OF THE VILLAGE GIVE THEMSELVES UP TO HEALTHIER PLEASURES. THEY HAVE NO PETRA OLEUM, BUT THEY ARE NOT SHORT OF IDEAS FOR CELEBRATING THE RETURN OF THE HEROES.
HAVE YOU EVER THOUGHT OF COOKING STUFFED BOAR?
?
COME ON, ASTERIX, TELL US ABOUT YOUR ADVENTURES!
WELL, IT ALL BEGAN IN THE QUIET, PEACEFUL DEPTHS OF THE GAULISH FOREST, WHERE EVERYTHING SEEMED TO INDICATE THAT IT WAS DINNER TIME...
SCRONTCH!
THE HOLIDAYS ARE OVER!
The End
UDERZO
8-81